ADVANCE PRAISE FOR

#BragOutLoud

"In clear, comforting, and honest language, Townsend encourages us to celebrate our accomplishments, big and small, and cheer each other on. There's no intensive, multi-day specialty diet—in 90 seconds a day, you can learn to honor yourself and support others and reclaim both community and self-appreciation in this harried existence that is modern life. The magic here is in engaging others in your own personal development. Want a more fulfilling, centered, balanced life? The key is the social solidarity Townsend taps into."

—**Tanya Cook**, Sociology Professor & Researcher

"This book is a must-read for anyone struggling with self-praise. I grew up with the expression 'self-praise is no recommendation' so learned early on to rely on external validation. This book, rightly so, turns that on its head! Self-praise is the best praise there is! The book is the gentlest 'how to' manual on how to get more joy, peace, happiness and all good things into our everyday lives."

—**Julia Bernard-Thompson**, TEDx Speaker and Business Coach

"Shannon Townsend has done it again! This book is as easy to read as her life-changing tools are to practice. #BragOutLoud is a must-read if you want to step out of the soul-crushing rat race, reclaim your inner spark, and finally feel good about who you are. It's simple, and it works."

—**Alexis Nair**, Award-winning Strategist

"The truth of this message resonates so loud that it cannot be stopped. It can no longer be denied. This is the new paradigm of thinking/being/

doing. An age-old concept has been turned upside down and Shannon prolifically demonstrates how we can all grow into more *joy* by embracing ourselves and the concept of bragging as a form of personal growth. This *is* the book you have been waiting for. You have been given permission to celebrate life and *yourself* to the fullest. Embrace it."

—**Rhonda Lee**, Creator of Spirit Mist Smokeless Smudge

"This book resonated strongly with me from page one. Shannon Townsend highlights why it's so normal to feel burned out and discouraged by your daily grind, but she also takes it a step further, and offers an (almost) too-simple-and-good-to-be-true solution. Her instructions will help you to reclaim ownership of the 'bright spots' in your daily life that have the capacity to refuel you and restore your outlook. If you've ever felt completely fed up with your actually pretty okay life and wondered 'why?!', then this is the book for you!"

—**Brynna Meraz**, Mom and Game Changer

"This fabulous book takes the universal idea of being more grateful and gives specific ideas and ways to create the necessary shift that gets you into the space to create and see major changes quickly. The magic happens when you . . . change how you feel in your core, in a powerful but simple way, and in under two minutes. Everyone can commit to two minutes a day to change their world."

—**Tracy Finkel**, CEO & Founder,
Designer at Breathing Gratitude

"Shannon Townsend has built a movement based on something so brilliant and profoundly life-changing, yet so simply and easily implemented. It allowed me to self-validate versus waiting for validation from others, something I'd struggled with my whole life."

—**Jae Haeri**, Author, Attorney and Business Coach

#BRAG OUT LOUD

THE SIMPLE SOLUTION TO FINDING MORE JOY

SHANNON TOWNSEND

Modern Wisdom Press
Boulder, Colorado, USA
www.modernwisdompress.com

Copyright © Shannon Marie Townsend, 2019

All rights reserved. No part of this book may be reproduced in any form without permission in writing from the author. Reviewers may quote brief passages in reviews.

Published 2019
Cover design by Karen Sperry Design
Author's photo courtesy of Emma Bauso Designs

ISBN: 978-1-951692-01-8 (paperback)

DISCLAIMER

No part of this publication may be reproduced or transmitted in any form or by any means, mechanical or electronic, including photocopying or recording, or by any information storage and retrieval system, or transmitted by email, without permission in writing from the author.

Neither the author nor the publisher assumes any responsibility for errors, omissions, or contrary interpretations of the subject matter within.

No part of *#BragOutLoud* may be reproduced or taught in any form or by any means without permission in writing from the author.

MEDICAL DISCLAIMER

The information in this book is a result of years of practical experience by the author. This information is not intended as a substitute for the advice provided by your physician or other healthcare professional. Do not use the information in this book for diagnosing or treating a health problem or disease, or prescribing medication or other treatment.

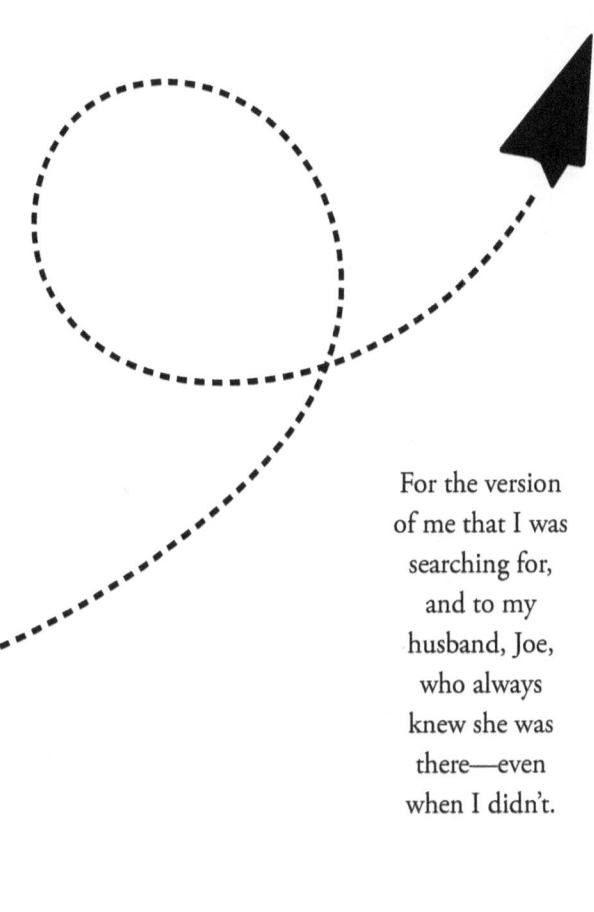

For the version of me that I was searching for, and to my husband, Joe, who always knew she was there—even when I didn't.

#CONTENTS

	Introduction	1
Chapter 1	Living an Unedited Life	5
Chapter 2	The Birth of #BragOutLoud	11
Chapter 3	90 Seconds A Day	21
Chapter 4	A Cultural Revolution	25
Chapter 5	What Does "Brag" Mean?	33
Chapter 6	Bragging in Action	39
Chapter 7	The Tough Stuff	47
Chapter 8	Brags and Inspiration	53
Chapter 9	What Does "Celebration" Mean?	63
Chapter 10	Dancing in the Kitchen	69
Chapter 11	Celebrations and Inspiration	73
Chapter 12	What if I Don't Have a Brag?	81
Chapter 13	Obstacles on the Path	101
Chapter 14	The Finish Line	107
	About the Author	111
	Further Reading	112
	Acknowledgments	115
	Thank You	117

#INTRODUCTION

I hope you picked up this book and scoffed, just a bit. I mean, who wouldn't?! We're taught from an early age to not brag, because if we do, we'll get too big for our britches.

We're told we'll be called conceited or rude, look like a fool, or claim ownership over things we have absolutely no right to. No one wants to be labeled as arrogant or snotty, or out of touch with reality.

No one wants to risk seeming boastful by proclaiming they've lost five pounds, or to get excited over something as silly as getting a new sponge. (Why would *anyone brag about that!?*)

As adults, we've learned well to keep it quiet—to censor ourselves, to share just the right amount of good, crummy, and mundane to not rock the boat. But our lessons in censoring ourselves started long before we became "real adults" on the morning of our 18th birthday.

We saw little Susie, bragging about her new dress, new toys, *and* her A+, and we didn't like her anymore. We didn't like her anymore because she took her brags and used them as weapons. Susie might not have even realized it at the time, but we did. We could hear in Susie's voice that her A+, her pristine toy, and her new dress were given to her because she deserved them and *clearly*, we hadn't earned them.

We started to self-censor as kids, before we ever realized it. We learned very quickly to tell our caregivers about the A on the spelling test or how far we got on the monkey bars, but only once a week. If we spoke up more than once on the same topic, we'd be labeled as conceited. How else could we interpret the eye roll or hearing our loved ones say, "You already told me about your spelling test"?

We learn to self-censor when we hear the well-meaning advice of adults we love say, "Now, don't wave your gift in front of all the other kids, that's not very nice." We have no choice but to internalize the message of "don't rock the boat"—you might just annoy or hurt someone with your small joy.

The evidence that bragging is the same as showing off and mean, *or* that it's conceited, only grows the older we get. We can't be too excited about getting first chair, acing that test, making the team, getting out of detention, going on a family vacation, getting a raise, getting a promotion, landing a bonus, or … the list goes on and on.

Until, one day, we're sitting with a friend chatting, and we realize: "I'm gonna burst if I don't tell someone!" Before we can ever share, the litany of reasons to hold back starts:

What if I tell her about the raise and she thinks I'm bragging?

What if I tell her about the promotion and she feels bad for not getting one, too?

What if I say it wrong and I sound conceited?

What if she thinks I didn't earn it?

I don't want her to feel bad or awkward!

If she tells Barbara, *everyone will know* and I *definitely* don't want that!

Ugh, I can't tell her that, she's got it so much harder than me.

The litany is so well rehearsed, we hardly recognize it.

Have you ever found yourself thinking, "I don't want to sound like I'm complaining, but I'm really bummed about this and *I know, I know, people have it worse*, but—first-world problems are still problems, right!?" Thoughts like this are just as bad and they're ingrained. We've been holding back for so long, we hide the good, the bad, the mundane, and the reality of our complicated and full lives, without questioning it.

That, my friend, is the real problem. We're so busy censoring ourselves for sounding conceited, whiny, or unappreciative that we are wearing ourselves out—but it doesn't have to be that way.

We really can share openly, our good *and* our struggles, without having to ditch all of our current friends (unless you want to, of course). We really can live an uncensored life and have others join in, without the world coming to an end. Without being labeled as stuck up, or worse, ungrateful.

This old way of minimizing the good in our lives has led us to hold back, not just in what we say out loud, but also in experiencing real joy. We can turn the old way of self-censoring on its head, without hurting anyone. We can create more small joys more often instead of portioning out joy after we've "earned" it.

The path to more joy is simple and it starts by reclaiming a tiny four-letter word: "Brag." Now, you can brag too, and I promise by the end of this short book, you'll have mastered how to brag and have time, energy, and focus to spare.

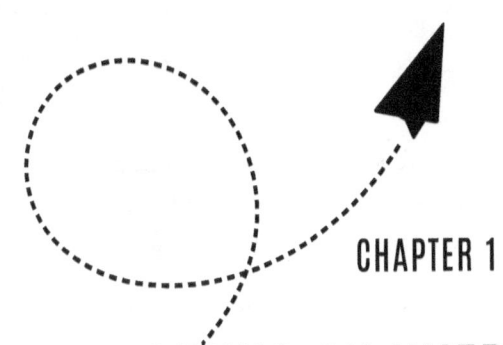

CHAPTER 1
LIVING AN UNEDITED LIFE

I've always felt that, especially as women, we have this shared bond of censorship. We're taught from an early age to mind our words, because if we don't, there will be consequences. Severe consequences, like parental disapproval, loss of friends, or worse, isolation and ridicule.

Most of us fall in line without realizing it, making sure we're the right balance of humble, brave, and right. *Or* we rebel and speak out as loudly and brazenly as possible. We end up screaming either way, either on the inside or outside, because the burden of projecting the perfect persona is killing us.

This isn't new information—great leaders have been speaking on this topic for generations—but what I've seen in my practice, working as a coach with business owners over the last five years, is the impact. This way of life just won't cut it anymore: We're exhausted, burned out, self-medicating with expensive coffee and wine, craving the weekend, and slowly realizing that we're not willing to put up with it anymore. If we keep it up, we're going to explode.

You can feel it in the air, this desire to drop the burden and be able to openly share about our lives—all of our lives. It's not about sharing your deepest darkest secret or only sharing the highs. It's the ability to share the ebb and flow of life with more than a select few people or your single "person."

We just want to be able to speak. To share the full spectrum of our lives, not just the hand-selected sections we've obsessed over that paint us in the right light, at the right time, in the right place.

Even reading that sentence is exhausting. The strain is palpable.

It's even harder when you've got a good life. When life is good, everyone expects to see the average highlights. No one wants to hear you brag *or* complain, because we've been raised to stay small, and we don't want anyone to feel hurt by our highs or jealous of comparative lows. Without realizing it, we frame all of our news with details to make our lives more palatable to the world. So our good or bad news sounds more like this:

A new (used) car

A (sensible) vacation

Cute (but poorly lit) family photos

A new dishwasher (because the old one broke)

We justify the good by making it average and therefore more acceptable.

If we go much beyond that, people start to judge our worthiness. We have this narrative, that others will judge whether you've *earned the life upgrade* or worse, whether you've had enough good in your life to suffer a loss. The world is watching, to see if those scales stay balanced—so you'd better be careful what you say.

If you share too much good, you'll get the scoff and eye roll. If you complain, it will be measured against your good: Do you have too much good to be allowed to grumble? Or, have you had too much bad, so now you're just wallowing?

We already know the hyper-vigilance of our personas is driving us to second-guess most everything we share about our lives. It's keeping us small, it's limiting our joy, and it's reinforcing a set of normal behaviors that is toxic to growth, satisfaction, and ease.

Here's the thing: It doesn't have to work like that. I have proof.

We can be ourselves, the uncensored versions, without being mean, uncaring, or clueless to the problems in the world. We can do it and still feel safe. It's possible to live in this new world, not in tiny secluded pockets, but every day, out loud, and in the open. I know this because I did a personal experiment in "uncensoring" my life and experienced dramatic increases in my energy levels, my ability to focus, my sense of joy, and my appreciation for the small things I did every day (as well as the small things done by those around me, like my husband). I couldn't believe the changes—there was no way it was this easy to live uncensored. When clients and friends started to comment on the difference, I knew it was time to take my experiment to a larger community.

I started a community the easiest way I knew how, with a new Facebook group. I popped in a graphic, the basic *How to #BragOutLoud*, and shared it with my clients and friends. They were used to seeing the hashtag in my personal posts, seeing the results, witnessing firsthand how much more energy I had, and they were eager to feel the same way.

We started with a 30-day goal of a single daily #BragOutLoud post each, and in under 72 hours, 50 people had joined me. We took off on September 1, 2017. The results poured in and after 30 days, we all knew that we had to keep going and spread the word.

We were taking as little as 90 seconds a day to change everything. It felt like we were changing the world, because we were. We had more patience for the daily grind, more energy to get through the day, and soon, we were all experiencing more joy—more joy, more often, and on a deeper, more refueling level. We had changed our world and it hadn't taken a miracle, a change in world leaders, or a winning lottery ticket (though that happened, too). The world was different, because we made it that way.

We had created a world where we shared our biggest accomplishments without fear. There was finally a world where we could grumble (even when we had really great lives and there were tons of people who would have traded to be in our place) and not be thought of as greedy or ungrateful. There was now a world where we can brag about our new kitchen sponges at the same moment someone else is suffering a great loss and *no one feels unheard, unseen, unloved, unappreciated, or guilty.*

Before you freak out about what kind of change this will require, I promise it's possible. It's possible, it's simple, and you can do it.

This won't be like the gratitude journal you started years ago and lost interest in (it happens, no judgment here). This isn't going to take a two-hour ritual, total silence, and the concentration of a laser beam.

You'll come back to this practice over and over again. This is your manual. (Good thing it's compact, right?!) You'll have mastered this practice by the end of the book, and once you're done, all you need is 90 seconds a day. You'll only need 90 seconds because if it took any longer, you wouldn't have time. You'll only need 90 seconds, because it doesn't take any longer than that to change your whole world.

First, I'm going to break down two words, reconstruct them, and then show you how to combine them. Then, you'll take as little as 90 seconds a day to radically change your world.

You won't need academic style notes, you won't need hours upon hours of practice. All you have to do is turn the page and get started. I'm with you all the way.

Ready?

CHAPTER 2

THE BIRTH OF #BRAGOUTLOUD

#BragOutLoud was a natural progression of experiences that took me from clueless and stumbling, scrambling for solutions, to examining what was going on for clients in my coaching practice, as well as many others I knew and loved.

It took me a long time to realize what the problem was. My clients were showing up overwhelmed and barely surviving. But it wasn't just entrepreneurs, it was moms, creatives, women in white-collar jobs. It was my friends. It was the women I loved and cared about deeply. I was overwhelmed, too. We were all trying to stave off weariness, even though on the whole, life was good. We were generally happy, but something was getting in the way of really *feeling* that. I knew I could support them (and me), but how?

"Maybe it's time management?" I wondered. So I created tools for creating schedules. And they worked! For a bit.

Then I thought, "It's gotta be organization!" So I created system after system to take the feeling clients had of being overwhelmed and turned it into an action plan. The systems worked—until they didn't.

Then I thought, "Alright—we need to eliminate the mental chatter that gets in the way!" So I created the Subliminal Focus Track. And it worked! It worked really well, but only if you used it consistently.

Even I forgot to use it regularly unless I had reminders in my calendar to play it while I worked, which I often found myself ignoring. That meant that the problem was bigger than I realized. For some reason, none of us were using the tools at our disposal consistently enough to accomplish our goals, even when those tools were effective and pretty effortless.

Burnout

In the meantime, I was feeling the same weariness that had crept into my soul when I had worked as a sign language interpreter. The burnout I'd experienced as an interpreter had been so slow and normal, I didn't take it seriously. Every interpreter I knew was struggling with balancing a schedule, getting the right continuing education, developing hobbies and a social life, and dealing with the competing needs of the interpreter as: 1. the communication expert and 2. the human behind the expert.

I'd left interpreting because I couldn't provide solutions. Legally, as well as ethically, I wasn't allowed to give my opinion or interject with solutions. I was the communication expert, not the problem fixer. I was also *very* sick and didn't know it. I'd been sick for months, but because of a million reasons, a simple problem had gone untreated.

It wasn't until I landed in the emergency room with intense pain and probably the flu that I realized how bad it had become. I know, don't go to the ER for the flu; I just wanted to know what was wrong with me and maybe get a bag of IV fluids. It was Saturday night on a holiday weekend. My doctor wouldn't be available for days and I needed answers now.

It wasn't the flu. I had a raging kidney infection that had been brewing for *months!* I was so burned out from work that I'd ignored my health. I ignored my health just like everyone else does, because I was too tired to do anything other than keep trudging along and zone out whenever I could. I'd been too stuck in survival mode to take care of myself and no job, no matter how much I loved it, was worth it. That's when I found myself sitting in bed weeks later, finally feeling better, realizing: "It's time to make a change."

Within a week, I had walked away from interpreting and moved full-time into coaching. Now I was able to take this passion for coaching I'd been working on for a couple of years and get my hands dirty. I could finally share my thoughts, craft solutions with clients instead of staying removed from the situation, and see the results through to the end. I was in my element, healthier than I had been in years, with more energy—and I was excited about going to work again!

Problem solved. Clearly, the problem had been the job setting (hint: It wasn't).

Except that, within a few years, I was feeling the burnout, the weariness, and the grumpiness seeping in. Just like I'd experienced with interpreting. I started getting sick again. I was sliding back into exhaustion, distractions around every corner, and apathy. *It should have been different!* I was giving clients brilliant solutions and they were making huge strides, but they weren't staying happy, either. How could good solutions not work? How could this much productivity not mean more joy and energy?

I'd been spending almost all of my coaching time cheerleading for others—reminding them of how great they were, how far they'd come, and the *absolutely massive changes they'd made*, but the joy from those leaps was fleeting. All the encouraging words, all the kudos, were genuine. But I was running out of steam. How could these inspiring and driven people *not see* how amazing they were? Why was their joy so fleeting, so easily forgotten?

The "Too Good" Life

In an effort to stall my own burnout, I started to reach out to the people in my life that were natural beacons of joy. Being in their presence helped, but it wasn't enough. Until one day, I was chatting with an old interpreter friend and several things clicked into place.

We had been chatting over coffee for a while when I realized she'd skirted the same issue a few times. I asked her what she was holding back on.

She blurted, "I can't say this to anyone else but you—but we just got an unexpected check! This money means we can replace our floors with what I wanted, get the *big* swing set I really want, *and* take a weekend trip with the kids."

My immediate response was explosive joy! She'd been talking about new floors, the swing set, and wanting a weekend road trip for a while. They could afford these things, but not all at once. She'd also said countless times, "The floors are fine. We don't really *need new ones*, I'd just really like different ones," and "We can go to the park, I know they'll grow out of the swing set, but I'd love that for them, but *we don't need it*." I also knew that several people had already scoffed at her desire for these and other life upgrades. She didn't need them—she wanted them.

She felt the world's judgment against that balance: too much good to "complain" and too much good to share more good fortune. She was stuck.

I squealed in delight for her. There was no worthiness quota she needed to reach to have good fortune, in my opinion. "You should be screaming this from the rooftops! I'm so happy for you," I gushed.

We discussed how blessed she felt and how she couldn't tell anyone else, because it would make people jealous (*"I wish I had random checks just show up in the mail"*), she'd appear ungrateful (*her flooring was fine*), she'd look snobby (*the swing set was actually a small fortress perfect for adventures*), she'd hate to look wasteful with money (*"You should invest, not waste it on things you don't actually need"*), and she would look greedy if she didn't donate more (*there are so many people who are less fortunate and might deserve it more*).

Everything she said made sense and was "normal," but it broke my heart that her good fortune had to be kept quiet. Her life was "too good" to have "earned" more good things happening.

Bright Spots

Within the same conversation, we talked about the time we worked together at an elementary school as classroom interpreters. We were part of a large team, spanning several grades. Our work was hard. Each student was at least two grades behind, in an underfunded district, and they all had aggressive educational goals. We worked our tails off.

Trying to stave off burnout was paramount. Stewing about whatever struggle we'd encountered that day would only end in a dismal day. Instead of falling into that predictable pattern, we made a simple choice. As a team, we waited for everyone in our storage-closet-sized office at the end of the day. We'd go around the circle and share a "bright spot" from the day. Some days, you'd have to pass—the day had been too stressful to have anything good immediately spring to mind—but eventually everyone had an example of how the day had been successful. Often times, one person's bright spot would inspire the others in the room, or the person who needed to pass, or a second share on days we really needed it. We'd support each other as best we could, never ignoring the real struggle—the work left to be done. The mountains we were all climbing were real *and* grueling and we *still* made a concentrated effort to mine the day for the bright spot that made it worthwhile. Even if that was, "I made it to the bathroom before PE class!" There was no hierarchy. Just a search for a small bubble of joy. It made all the difference in the world during the hardest days and expanded our joy on lighter days.

I lamented not having a group of people to do bright spots with, and how valuable that had been for everyone's mental health. And then it clicked.

My friend should be able to share her financial windfall as a bright spot and everyone should just accept it, allow it to be, without judgment. She shouldn't have to edit what she shares just because the world was unjustly measuring her.

"I don't want to brag, it's not worth it," my friend said. "I get it," I sympathized, "but it's not right. You should be able to brag. You're not trying to rub it in anyone's face. Your intentions are good."

The Fleeting "Yay!" Moments

I spent the next several days examining client comments, previous jobs, and all the stories I'd heard, and realized that the problem wasn't as simple as I'd thought at coffee with my friend, but the solution *was* deceptively easy.

Everyone around me—clients, friends, collaborators, mentors—*everyone* was missing the opportunity to celebrate their minor wins, their big wins. The "Yay!" of their lives was too fleeting. The "Yay!" of their lives wasn't lasting long enough to refuel them. The "Yay!" was hardly ever recognized, let alone basked in.

What was so astounding to me was that regardless of where I was, the people around me were doing extraordinary things: mastering new technology, raising tiny compassionate warriors, getting to work, setting up businesses, going back to school, growing their marriages, dissolving partnerships, and growing their businesses by 200 percent and tripling their income. Yet, they were all suffering as if they'd accomplished nothing.

The problem wasn't their work ethic, it wasn't their circumstances growing up, and it wasn't their profession. Their burnout and their exhaustion were born from a place of needing to always "do more" and censoring their moments of accomplishment (not that they realized that, or that I did either). They lacked joy. It was rampant, and worse, it was expected and accepted.

The long-suffering artist, the stressed caregiver, and the overwhelmed entrepreneur are all-too-common tropes. No one could celebrate their tiny wins, because if you celebrated every time you did the dishes, or got the kids to school, or passed a test, or parked in a good spot—well, people would think you were, what? Silly, faking it, trying too hard?

Even worse, if you celebrated the big wins, you might make someone feel—jealous? Like they don't measure up? What if people thought you didn't deserve it or were ungrateful?

Two Small Words

And then it dawned on me. I realized that if we reclaimed two small words—"brag" and "celebrate"—and practiced them consciously together, there was a chance we could radically shift the inner dialogue we use to censor ourselves and possibly refuel our bone-weary bodies and overworked brains at the same time.

So I tried it. I reclaimed those two little words. I redefined "brag" and "celebrate" to reflect a deeper sense of recognition and rest. I tried, I fumbled, and I practiced with these new definitions for 30 days straight.

The results were spectacular and shocking. I had more energy. I had deeper focus. I had become a safe place for so many other peoples' stories. I had rocked the boat, but no one fell overboard. I felt safe in this new world I'd created.

The cliché of being a wildly different person didn't apply to me. The world felt different. I felt different, but I wasn't a different person. I was who I wanted to be more frequently and for longer and longer periods of time. I was more of the Shannon I wanted to be, and my inner dialogue allowed me to stop censoring myself, without hurting anyone.

And the bonus was that in 30 days, I felt more anchored, joyful, and open. I still had the same spectacular life as before, but I didn't feel guilty when I talked about it anymore. I no longer felt like my joy would bother other people. I knew I was talking about the ups and downs of my life without being pompous (like I'd always assumed it would be perceived). I wasn't on that razor edge of burnout like before.

My life wasn't wildly different. I wasn't wildly different.

I didn't want a completely different life. I wanted to enjoy my life more easily and still be me. I wanted to stop portioning out joy for sporadic and worthy occasions and all of a sudden, I was. I wanted to keep my good life and when things got hard (as they always do), I wanted to be able to get through it without feeling guilty for hitting a rough patch. I didn't need to be a wildly different person (and neither do you) to feel more joyful.

My capacity for joy had grown exponentially. Which meant that I was less tired and cranky. I could give more freely, because there was more to give. I'd often experienced a sort of "joy whiplash" after a big positive event (e.g. getting a raise, enjoying a girl's day, landing a new client). Carrying that much joy would leave me exhausted afterwards. The whiplash I often felt after a big, exciting, joyful moment lessened, because joyful was more common. I got used to more joy, so my endurance for joy skyrocketed and I had twice the energy at the end of each day.

My inner dialogue became geared towards mining for the good, in a genuine and meaningful way. I was pulling out of minor funks in record time. I was more focused in my business than I had been in ages. My relationship felt stronger. And people were starting to notice, well before the end of my 30-day trial run.

People were starting to echo back the language I was using. All of a sudden, people were asking me how they could celebrate their small accomplishments. Clients were starting conversations with, "I just gotta brag on myself for this." Family even started using "hashtag brag out loud" in conversation.

My first 30 days weren't just focused on the highlights. I had several serious setbacks in that time, and I was able to utilize them, not wallow in them. I lost a contract that was lucrative, I felt down and sad, I got into a major argument with my husband, and I wasn't selected for a speaking gig. I grew from the setbacks, I grieved their potential and my disappointment, *and* I found my bright spot in record time. I didn't *rush* through those setbacks; I *grew* through them.

I appreciated that losing the contract made space for someone better suited. The argument with my husband meant I had to confront a failing on both sides and try better. Not getting the speaking gig just felt hard and so did feeling sad, but the bright spot was that they were survivable, that I could witness my own disappointment and pain without getting lost in it. Experiencing all of this in such a short period of time made me a better listener, a stronger leader, and a more self-compassionate human.

When it was time to invite people into the #BragOutLoud community, I had the basics down. I had the framework (which we'll cover in the next chapters) in hand and ready to share. I had the capacity to bear witness to everything from getting excited over a new broom to grieving the loss of a pet or the dissolving of a relationship to celebrating promotions and raises. I could share and hear "silly" moments and "serious" shares without the hierarchy of worthiness I'd internalized while growing up.

Reclaiming two tiny words had begun to change people's lives, without ever changing their individual circumstances. Whether they already had a "good life" or were "knee deep in the struggle," the results were the same. Having permission to brag and celebrate led to more genuine connection, feeling heard for possibly the first time ever, and more endurance for joy.

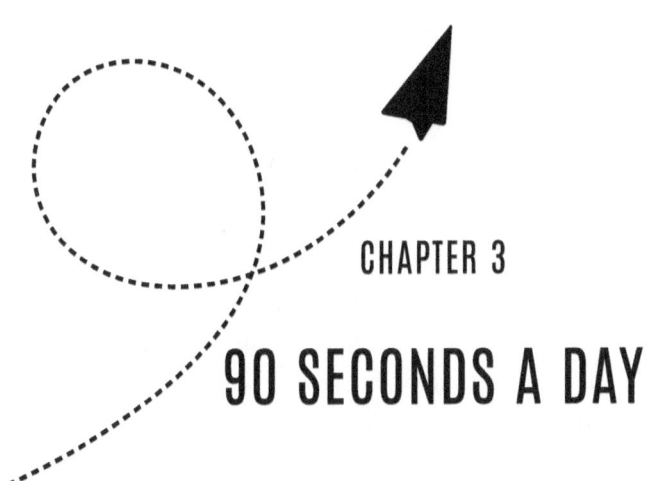

CHAPTER 3

90 SECONDS A DAY

The process of #BragOutLoud is simple, deceptively so.

In the chapters ahead we'll reclaim what it means to *brag* and *celebrate*. We're going to redefine these two words, so that we can be more of ourselves, more often.

We are going to be cultivating a daily practice in a safe space. A safe space is one where you may still feel nervous or unsure, but you know that if you stumble, you'll be supported, not ridiculed. Once you're in a safe space (whether that's with your closest friends, online with us, or sitting in bed at the end of the day with your thoughts), you'll be reviewing your day and finding the simplest, easiest, and fastest example of your greatness. In the beginning, you'll have a moment that jumps out as your day's highlight. Great!

You can use that simple moment. *Or* a moment you would normally have ignored as not important enough. *Or* a moment you'd normally feel too embarrassed to share (those are my favorite).

You'll be able to do the entire #BragOutLoud process in as little as 90 seconds. Faster than any other process I know of, with exponentially bigger, brighter, and more satisfying results. Promise.

New Definitions

Before we redefine these words in the next chapters, let's take a look at what a #BragOutLoud moment can look like. We think we already understand what "brag" and "celebrate" mean, and that these words must be used in conjunction with big, noteworthy occasions, but does your definition fit the following examples?

I'm gonna #BragOutLoud about filling a bin of weeds from the garden. I celebrated by dancing up the stairs and flopping down on the couch for a breather.

OR

#BragOutLoud for finally getting my tires rotated. Celebrated by dancing in my kitchen while balancing a fresh cup of coffee.

OR

#BragOutLoud: I finally put the sympathy card in the mail today. I celebrated by eating the last cookie and taking two minutes to send some virtual love and support.

OR

Just gotta #BragOutLoud because today I learned it's normal to have one breast larger than other. (Guys have that too, for their bits, which I knew, but somehow missed the memo for women?!) Crazy I was "today years old" when I found out. Celebrated by taking a few deep breaths and telling my inner 12-year-old that we're normal.

See? Not so hard, not so serious, not so labor intensive, right?

It's really not, but I want to warn you: Don't skip ahead or leave this small tome unfinished. Each segment has a specific purpose that we'll dive into in the next couple of chapters. You'll see why it's easy to brag *or* celebrate, but it's paramount to do them together, one right after each other, to build up our stamina. I'd hate for you to not get the full benefit of our time together by not realizing how cultivating a brag *and* a celebration refuels and expands our capacity for joy.

Listen to Your Inner Voice

As you start reading and getting a feel for the #BragOutLoud universe, take the time to listen to what your inner voice is saying. If you've got questions, concerns, or fears, I want you to jot them down. Scribble them on a sticky note and stick it in the pages. I suppose you could scribble in the margins, highlight, dogear—it's your book! Make it work for you.

I want you to put your concerns down on paper. If you're worried about what your Mom would say, jot it down. If you're plagued by your inner voice insisting that you're being conceited or "too big for your britches," document it. Honor that part of your inner voice; she's there to protect you. Writing down your concerns helps you refocus. If you're busy arguing with your inner voice, you're not going to make much progress. Instead, get it out of your head and keep moving forward.

Jotting down your inner questions and conflict is great, since you're proving to your inner voice, your little gremlins, and the tapes on repeat in your mind that you *can* listen, you *can* find answers, and you *can* do it without hurting anyone's feelings!

Stick with me as we get the specifics down in the next few chapters, and you'll be rockin' and rollin' with your #BragOutLoud moments in no time!

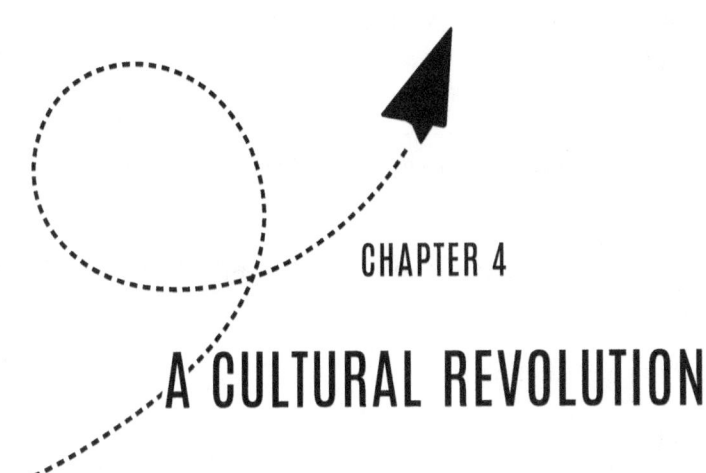

CHAPTER 4

A CULTURAL REVOLUTION

Culture is a set of normal behaviors, assumptions, and action, and it is the motivator and creator of almost every facet of our lives. It is the driving factor of 90 percent of our choices—it's no wonder that women find themselves falling into common narratives, all based on the cultural stories we've known our entire lives. Some of these narratives are beneficial, while others leave us feeling stuck and misunderstood. It's time we start deciding for ourselves what narratives we live out, and it all starts with the language we use.

Culture is based in language—the language we hear, the language we use, the language we grew up with—which means we're going to work slowly to incorporate new language until it feels natural.

The stories we hear and the expectations we learn to meet are how we're socialized. This is how we internalize the wider culture we grew up in. So what are the common narratives or tropes that drive our choices and options? If you've ever had to consider the following questions, you're struggling with how you've been socialized:

What should I wear?

What should I do in this uncomfortable situation?

What career opportunities should I pursue?

- # If I have family, what responsibilities will automatically be mine?
- # Should I expect my husband to change diapers/"babysit"/stay home?
- # Should I go out by myself?
- # Should I cut off all of my hair?
- # Should I live alone?
- # Should I wear more makeup? Less makeup?
- # Will these earrings make me look pretentious?
- # What if I decide to not get married? Not have children? Not work? Not do hot yoga?

This is language shaping our culture.

The deeper we go, the more familiar it feels. We live by a set of rules that we no longer think about: where we can walk, how we can address certain situations, what topics we can or can't talk about, if we can wear the same outfit twice in a week, what others will say about our food choices, our vices, our children. The list is never-ending. We're constantly in an internal dialogue with ourselves based on these *shoulds* and the expectations passed down to us.

These shoulds are all around us, influencing us in subtle ways. They slip out of our mouths as "Do you mind doing (some part of an already agreed upon commitment or job)?" or "Just an idea I had, you don't have to do anything with it!" or "Should I really eat that cake? Bathing suit season is almost here, ya know."

The narratives that are normal get mixed in with what we heard as children. Were you expected to be athletic? tough? demure? funny? attractive? thin? loud? smart? feminine? unobtrusive? perfect?

Narratives like "little girls wear pink" and "boys tug on our hair to show they like us" and "all girls gossip, but they shouldn't" illustrate to us what the world thinks we can or should do, expect, or tolerate. We can hear the voice in our minds telling us "don't do that," or feel the tummy flip if we show up somewhere less than prepared.

The tapes in our head are built on culture's expectations: the broader culture of where we grew up; our familial culture; and the situational culture of places like school, church, the grocery store, and work. Even our homes have cultural expectations. And if you're in a partnership, you get to compete with the expectations your partner developed, too.

Most of these expectations were handed to us, and the negative thought cycle we developed as a result has been wreaking havoc ever since. We didn't think one day, "You know, I really am horrible to look at." Those kinds of thoughts were created in the back of our minds, from bits and pieces of the culture we are surrounded by.

From the Inside Out

Knowing that culture is this massive, never-ending driving force, we're faced with a dilemma. Do we conform and lose ourselves, our voices, our energy, and make ourselves sick one way or another; or do we change the culture?

Conformity sounds boring, soul-crushing, and frankly—once we realize how deeply it goes, how often it has held us back—we realize that the exhaustion we feel every day is from holding back small pieces of ourselves. We held back, censored ourselves, most likely without realizing it, as a mechanism to stay safe and to be accepted by those around us. There's no shame in that. We crave acceptance and the associated comfort of being part of a group. We've lived this way our whole lives, but we can step away from the conformity and keep the safety and comfort we need. All we have to do is change the culture and our own internal dialogue. Even though changing the culture that surrounds us sounds like a *massive, massive* undertaking, it's possible. Even if you're grappling with the question, "How can we change the world when we can't even master our own inner dialogue?"

The answer is simple: We change our *inner* culture first.

We don't start with our global culture, our home nation's culture, or even our familial culture. We start by searching for that bright spot in our day and then amplify it with an intentional celebration. We nurture the part of us that has been desperate for the comfort of knowing we're not inherently broken.

This inner cultural shift amplifies gratitude practices, the deep calm that comes during and after yoga, the healing of therapy, and the connection we feel with our chosen family and pets. Our inner culture shifts when we claim our bright spots for what they are—brags—and then say them out loud.

Claim these brags for the world to see. Eventually. We'll work up to shouting from the rooftops one day. But it's crucial we hear ourselves speak these truths out loud first. Even in a whisper.

Just like when we buy a new red car, we see a million red cars; when we focus attention on our bright spots, our brags, the more of them we find. The more we find, the more normal they become. The more we mine our day for brags, the easier they are to see in the harder moments or the moments that are making us feel *extra* tired.

The Platinum Rule

At this point, most people say, "But ... if I start to really #BragOutLoud, that might hurt someone's feelings/make them uncomfortable/jealous. Doesn't that break the Golden Rule? I was raised to treat others how you wish to be treated, don't tell me that's wrong now. I certainly don't want to feel uncomfortable or jealous!"

Good point. So let's use the Platinum Rule instead: Treat others as *they wish to be treated*. It's a subtle shift from the Golden Rule and allows for a little more empathy, understanding, and compassion. The Platinum Rule is best illustrated for me when I'm sick versus when my husband is sick. My husband prefers to be cuddled, have no food, and read a book. For years, I couldn't figure out why he made me so angry when I was sick. It clicked one day when I realized that when I'm sick, I prefer to be left alone and not touched, have salty food on demand, and watch mindless TV that I don't have to think about. He was always trying to rub my back or find me a book, because that's what he would want, and the last thing I needed. Now when either of us is sick we take care of each other's needs. He sets up a spot on the couch for me to be left alone with salty snacks within reach. When he's sick, I make sure he's got a good book and comes to bed each night to get some much-needed cuddles.

Especially in the beginning, we're not going to be bragging in front of or to the people who will make it harder. We'll treat them as they wish to be treated and not share with them. We won't push on their inner dialogue, so they won't be triggered by our outer dialogue, our bragging.

We all deserve to feel safe. Unfortunately, bragging got a bad rap, and now listening to any kind of brag makes most people feel unsafe or uneasy. Instead of shoving our newfound idea down their throats, we'll cultivate our #BragOutLoud practice in a safe place (there's a community you can join to start practicing at the end of this book).

We want our intention and our impact to match up as often as we can. At first, our intent of trying to develop a stronger and gentler inner culture might have a negative impact, as doing so also tries to change the cultural narrative. Asking the people around us to change, naturally, causes some pushback. Until we normalize this practice, we'll practice where our intent and impact are guaranteed to match up, in our safe spaces.

Not Hard Work

The next concern I hear is, "Okay, but—I've had this inner voice, this inner culture, for a loooooong time, Shannon, so to change it is going to take *a lot* of work!"

Most hard things don't stick. Plus, *who has time for more hard things*? No one does—that's why #BragOutLoud is so easy.

Once you master the two parts (the brag and the celebration), you'll be able to whip one up in as little as 90 seconds. The point of #BragOutLoud was never to create more *work* for anyone; it was a daily tweak to start refueling those dangerously low tanks we have. It was an avenue for those with crummy days, those with "picture perfect" lives, and *average women* to increase their capacity for joy.

If we can carry more joy, we can change the world. It is time to make radical self-care accessible to the masses. It's radical to pause in our day and bask in our own glory. We're doing it because joy doesn't have to be spooned out in tiny doses. We can easily and radically cultivate more joy every day. Now it's time to make that intentional stop, that brag, a normal part of our day—make it less radical, more typical.

We're burned up and burned out. If we don't do something soon, we're gonna collapse and never fully recover.

It's time to refuel, in 90-second increments. It's time to do it in a community. It's time to transform our culture around being worn down and tuned out.

It's time, and you are ready.

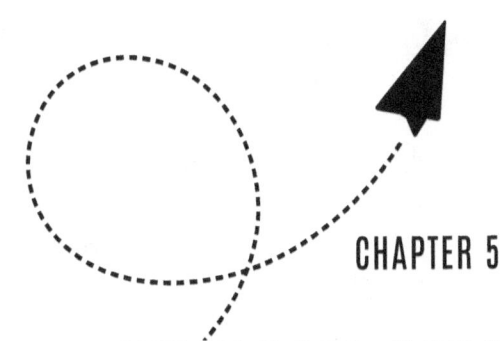

CHAPTER 5

WHAT DOES "BRAG" MEAN?

A brag in the new culture we're developing is defined as: recognition of a moment in time. That's it.

A single moment in time.

A moment. The moment can be anything. A moment has no classifiers, no requirements. No external demands to be *really* important, to change the world, or to save someone's life.

Brags can be "good": a raise, a completed to-do list, or a clean kitchen sink.

Brags can be "bad": having a hard day, getting fired, or stubbing your toe.

Holding good and bad brags at the same time is crucial! It's crucial because our days are not strictly good or bad, they are a mix. A mix worthy of recognizing, of normalizing.

We want good and bad on display. We want to see it.

Once we begin to recognize it in ourselves, we can start to see it in others. We can realize the person who cuts us off in traffic isn't an inherently terrible person. Maybe they're having a bad day, maybe they didn't see us, maybe they're rushing home to surprise their partner or kiddo with their favorite treat—maybe they're human, just like us.

Maybe once we can hold the good and the bad, we can be kinder to ourselves. I promise being kinder to ourselves will make this language transition a little easier because we're using it in the full scope of our lives—the good *and* the bad. A brag is still a brag regardless of that moment's size, scope, impact, or influence.

Any size: finding a lost sock, finding an uncashed check, or walking 10,000 steps.

Any scope: a personal secret triumph, a corporate team's new, record-breaking month, or a kindergarten's successful recital.

Any impact: saving a single earthworm from the sidewalk, sponsoring a local team, or being in charge of birthday cards at the office.

Any influence: rallying a group to walk a charity 5k, meeting and befriending your idol, or taking a small group of excited kids on their first camping trip.

We choose it. We can brag about anything and, because there is no hierarchy in brags, it all counts as a brag.

It doesn't matter how impressive the world finds any of the brags listed above or throughout this book; they are all equally important. They are all equally successful when it comes to bragging. They all check the "single moment in time" box.

Kind of an overwhelming realization, right? If there's no hierarchy, then there's almost too much to choose from. If brags can be good or bad, how do you even start? How do you begin to brag? It's like you get to have whatever flavor ice cream you'd like, but you have to choose it from every flavor known to the universe, and they are all laid out in front of you.

Instead of being overwhelmed by your options, try to choose a brag from a category. See, humans inherently love parameters, but hate rules. Which means I won't give you rules to brag by. I'll give you, let's say, sandboxes to play in.

Your sandboxes could be anything from experiences with other people, things you did or witnessed, to progressing on or surviving struggles in your personal life. They could be about your relationships, about work, or about your pets. There will be a nice list at the end of the chapter you can look through, and Chapter 12 is dedicated to even more sandboxes to explore.

The important thing about bragging is that once you land on something, you don't second-guess it. You brag boldly (in our safe space, remember) and with courage. Courageous brags do so many wonderful things for you: They provide increased confidence, more proof you're amazing, more joy, and they go a long way towards building up your depleted reserves. It's a subtle shift. You're easing into this, which means that instead of bashing yourself or anyone else over the head with #BragOutLoud, we're going to ease in.

We're going to change up the whole world without much effort at all, and it will be so natural that, pretty soon, you'll wonder why bragging was ever treated like a four-letter word.

Now It's Time to Start Bragging

You can start bragging at the dinner table with your family, at the start of a staff meeting, as part of catching up with friends, or you can join us online. We'll get deeper into why bringing others into #BragOutLoud is important, how community amplifies joy, and where to find that community in the next chapters.

You can brag about anything and everything, but if you draw a blank, here are some areas (or sandboxes) that could inspire you.

(There are more suggestions in Chapters 8 and 12.) You could #BragOutLoud about:

The simplest thing you did today.
Whatever you started in the last hour.
Your biggest accomplishment from yesterday.
Your smallest accomplishment from last week.
Your proudest moment of the year.
The award/acknowledgement from elementary school you only got to mention once. (No hierarchy or timeframe, remember?)
A moment that changed the trajectory of your life, no matter how long ago it was.
Your favorite gadget and what it does to make your life better.
Your pet's antics.
Your proudest moment of your loved ones, kids, family, or partner.
Your most recent life upgrade.
An intimate moment with a partner.
Your latest setback (and its deeper meaning/impact on your life).
The sweetest thing your partner did for you.
A big work accomplishment.

\# A small work accomplishment.

\# What you did at the end of a crummy day.

\# Your last vacation.

\# The book you just finished.

\# The meal you made.

\# Your cup of coffee's perfect hue.

\# Remembering to make it to the bank.

Jot some brags down and marvel at yourself. See? You *can* find something to brag about!

CHAPTER 6

BRAGGING IN ACTION

Learning to cheerlead for yourself is a journey, not a destination. It's okay if this feels funky or you don't think you're "doing it right." You are, I promise.

For me, it's all about the practice and the option (not obligation). I did it every day for nine months, but that's not the definition of perfect, of doing it right. It's just how it happened. The #BragOutLoud movement is about creating a restorative practice for *you*, not the gal down the street, or the dude at work.

You are learning a new skill set. You're reclaiming a word the world has a lot of opinions about. You are allowed to figure this out as you go.

We are practicing, together, a new way of looking at our days. A new way of thinking and speaking to ourselves. It's a minor shift, with radical results: more joy, more energy, and more self-compassion.

As we normalize this practice, which can take as little as 90 seconds, we're learning to cheer for ourselves. We are slowly and steadily building up our ability to hold joy for longer and longer periods of time. Mastering how to live uncensored means we're sharing the good *and* the struggles and celebrating all of it. Cheering isn't reserved for the perfect moment anymore; it's used to enliven us when we realize we knocked out our to-do list *or* when our to-do list knocked us down. The world may see that as cheering or complaining, but we know the difference now. Even if it feels like we don't have the hang of it yet.

This is allowed to take practice. You are allowed to stumble. *This is not a space where you make yourself feel bad and strive for perfection.*

Nothing within the #BragOutLoud movement has a hierarchy. Which means whatever you manage to accomplish or are able to do, could never be done "wrong." Every moment in your life can be a #BragOutLoud moment; regardless of size, scope, impact, or influence. It can be good, bad, or mundane. It all counts. It's all perfect.

The perfection already exists—you are just playing with it, which I hope is freeing.

Safe Spaces

When I start to espouse the value of sharing your brags (both good and bad) one of the many responses I get is, "Yeah, but—what if someone scoffs at my crummy day?! There are so many other people who have it worse. I can't win. I've either got it way better than other people and I'm ungrateful, or I shouldn't rub my good fortune in other people's faces because that's conceited."

Great point! That's why we *never, ever, ever* start this practice outside of an unsafe environment. We have a wonderful community online, but if that's not your style, grab a group of gals and read this book together. Pass this book to a like-minded friend, see how she feels. Snoop around online and see how others are using #BragOutLoud to live their unedited lives.

Above all else, start in a safe space so that you can try it out. Test the process, be inspired by others, and if you join our community, get support on how to claim both the brag *and* the celebration. Allow yourself to normalize this practice before you feel like you *have to* yell from the rooftops.

Having a safe space is why we can share our good brags and our bad brags, because the judgment doesn't exist here. We're all sharing to the best of our abilities. Everyone has their own path to an uncensored life. The safe space is created with intention, so that you can grow, practice, and cultivate joy more often.

My hope, and the hope of the larger #BragOutLoud movement, is that you'll get so used to this practice, you won't be able to stop yourself. You'll naturally start speaking this way. You'll naturally use this framework in your everyday language.

You'll end up practicing this, feeling the shift for yourself, and by then very few people would be bothered to scoff or comment. Most will be too busy cheering you on, because you've figured out how to share your unedited life in a way that inspires more joy and connection.

Supported By and Supporting Your Community

Bragging out loud in a safe space also has astounding impacts on the community at large. Whether you cultivate a #BragOutLoud culture at work, in your family unit, or with your close friends, it reinforces the safety of communities by sharing vulnerability and personality and creating genuine connections. The community is reinforced by your courage and the individuals in the community gain inspiration, examples, and a broader vision.

Within the online #BragOutLoud community, we've witnessed

a vast range of brags: secret weddings, life upgrades (a new trash can), health (final cancer treatments), intimacy (saying "I love you"), family transitions (moving, elder care, palliative care), financial windfalls, risk (investments in all manner of things), pets, kids, and so many others.

The community always grows *with you* as you brag, because they are inspired to see their own lives a little differently. A community member might have had a similar experience, and your brag reminds them to share and brag too.

One of the most heart-expanding experiences I've had with the community is my own ability to bear witness to the *realness* of others' lives—to witness people take a moment and brag about something that is challenging.

One community member bragged: "We made the decision to move my father into elder palliative care so he can be more comfortable, and we can be with him as family, loving him deeply, without being his caretakers. We're celebrating his life and our choice to do this with a sheet cake and hugs." The outpouring for that brag wasn't one of grief, commiseration, or the sadness you'd expect. It was a loving support of prioritizing the comfort and care of *everyone in that situation*. A deep honoring of everyone's needs—in a hard, hard time.

The community held space and honored so much more of that situation than you'd expect. Celebrating with her, as she made a hard choice. And because the community is reinforced by these *very real* life experiences, we could bear witness without the need to live differently. We could be with her in spirit and still brag about the new trash can, the antics of a grandchild, or the choice to donate to a favorite charity.

With no hierarchy, we're free to have a full range of experiences, take that moment of recognition, and build from there. We start to normalize this range of human experience.

It's easy for me to say, "There's no hierarchy, don't worry, just find the good" and walk away, but I promise it's true, if not a little challenging on the face of it. We've grown up in a culture that says, "Everything has a hierarchy; you can't hold space for both a new trash can and palliative care, as one is clearly more important than the other and to suggest otherwise would be disingenuous and hurtful."

That's just it, though—we're not diminishing any of these aspects of our lives, we're simply pausing to reflect on them, to take what we can from all of these moments. To find genuine joy as often as we can. When we divorce an arbitrary scale of worthiness from these very real situations, we're free to feel them however we need to.

Maybe that means we sit in fear or relief, whether that's fear the wind will whip our new trash can away or the relief of passing medical care to someone who's more experienced so that we can focus on our own feelings, without the responsibilities of being the sole caretaker of a terminally ill relative.

It's okay if this new non-hierarchy feels weird to you, if you feel uncomfortable at first. We're changing our internal culture, the language we use every day to reflect our intention to pause, recognize, and normalize all that it means to be a human being.

What about the things we aren't able or ready to find the bright spot in? What if it feels complicated to sit with, let alone #BragOutLoud about? What if it feels like there's nothing positive at all? We'll dive deep into what to do when you encounter "Tough Stuff" in

Chapter 7 and what to do if you draw a total blank in Chapter 12, titled "What if I Don't Have a Brag?"

Regardless, know that the moment you start to wrestle with these issues, you're doing it right. You're getting what you need out of #BragOutLoud. You're taking an honest look at life, in all its messy glory. You're learning to bear witness to all of life, and that is a skill you'll hone and work on your whole life long.

We're trying to normalize the process of bragging, to pause and recognize a single moment in time, the good and the bad. We begin to heal through witnessing what's really entertaining, what's really challenging, and what's mundane. It all counts. It's all worthy, and there's a freedom in that.

This is how we change our community culture, our familial culture. We make it normal for ourselves and then make it normal for our extended circles of influence.

If we can normalize this powerful practice for ourselves, it becomes a natural extension of our everyday lives. We internalize this new way of moving through the world and it slowly but surely transforms our inner dialogues. When our inner dialogues change, our outer dialogues change, too.

We naturally begin to speak about our brags. It's subtle. Even if we end up bragging about crummy circumstances or hard times, we brag about the good stuff too. Slowly we change how we speak to those around us, because how we're speaking to ourselves has changed.

The people around us notice this nuanced change and mimic it back to us.

Redefining Normal

What do you do in the meantime? What if you feel silly or it feels *almost like you might just be lying to yourself?*

What if that bright spot is tiny? Or mundane? Or you're trying too hard to find a bright spot at all? You're not alone in feeling like it might be challenging. That awkward feeling is just you, redefining what's normal for you.

These feelings of getting acclimated are *totally the most normal human thing ever.* Ever.

How cumbersome did it feel when you learned to drive? What about learning to kiss? Did you feel like you'd mastered these things immediately? I didn't.

#BragOutLoud didn't feel normal at first, either. There were days when it felt like I was trying *really, really hard* to find a brag at all. And let's be honest, I still feel that way sometimes.

Some days it feels a bit silly. And when it does, I try my hardest to realize it, shrug, and keep going. Keep bragging, even when it feels a bit hokey. Sometimes, it still feels cheesy, no matter how we spin it. On the days that feels true, we laugh to ourselves and try again tomorrow.

Some days it felt too easy and it would have been far too easy to ignore my good days as "normal" and not #BragOutLoud at all. It's all normal. All part of redefining a new normal for you. As long as your intention is breaking free from the cultural burden to be perfect, humble, *and* happy, it's all just fine.

Consistency is Great and Forgetting is Normal

The last piece of learning to brag for ourselves is to realize: Consistency is great and forgetting is normal. My nine-month streak ended because one day I forgot. The day got away from me (in the best way) and all of a sudden—I'd not done my #BragOutLoud in four days. Of course, when this happened, I did the same thing everyone else does: I beat myself up.

How could I just forget?! How could I not be perfect in my execution of this practice that's all about ditching perfection, embracing the full scope of life, and increasing my capacity for joy?

Then I remembered—I'm human, too. I'd told countless community members, "It's okay, we all forget. It happens. So, *so*, thrilled you came back—that's a brag all on its own, how can we celebrate with you?!"

It would be great if you finished this book, joined the #BragOutLoud Movement, and never missed a day. However, that has never been my goal for you.

It's enough if you #BragOutLoud once a week, once a year, or four times a day for three days straight. This is a lifestyle change. This is a *movement*. This is a practice you will come back to over and over again. And because it can take you as little as 90 seconds a day, I really hope you find it easy to incorporate and even easier to jump back in when you fall off the wagon.

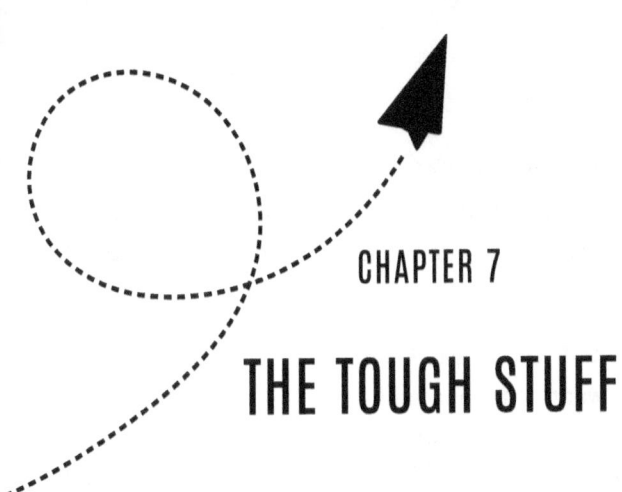

CHAPTER 7

THE TOUGH STUFF

Once we've played around with the #BragOutLoud concept for a while, we often stumble onto days that require a lot more digging to find the good. We find ourselves in a deeper funk, wondering why there doesn't seem to be an easy way to turn our brags around and feel better about them. We start hiding from cultivating a #BragOutLoud, or we feel guilty for not contributing to our #BragOutLoud community.

This is normal. Getting through those days requires a new framework, one that honors our needs and the realities of going through or witnessing the tough stuff.

Underdog Days

Our dominant culture loves the comeback/underdog success story. We are fanatical about the rags-to-riches plot, because it means "I could overcome, too." But we only love it if the underdog wins. If the underdog doesn't make a comeback, we're less interested. This narrative drives us to only share what's really going on once we've triumphed, once we've overcome.

We hide our stories of the *process of coming back*, of *striving*, of *trying* until we've won and proven we're worthy of creating our own comeback story. To this day, I still look at my underdog days (they happen even though I've got a *fantastic* life; some days just feel crummy) and try and figure out how to make a compelling comeback story out of them. To skip over the crummy bits and only highlight how I overcame.

I don't want to admit that I avoided applying for a speaking opportunity. I don't want to say out loud that upon learning I needed a polished speaker reel instantly made me cry because I don't have one. (Oh, and plus, I haven't reached my goal weight, so, no, I'd rather *not be on a video* that I can't afford to make anyway, for your event that's happening three states over.) I cringe when I realize I distracted myself so much, I ended up missing the deadline. Nope. I'd much rather espouse the virtue of "stick-to-it-ness," of persevering, getting through all those roadblocks, and being asked to speak at the event—all because "I wouldn't let distractions get in my way."

Doesn't that sound better? More worthy of celebration, of claiming, of sharing? Perseverance and triumph sound more like the soundbites I'm used to.

But admitting to *all* of the struggle is more human. I did distract myself away from applying for that keynote speaker gig. I did cry and eat all my feelings (and then cried again when I told my husband about it). I glossed over it and hid from that story, until I realized I could stop the spiral of feeling horrible by sharing. I hadn't overcome. I'd failed my own goal. This wasn't the first time it had happened, and it certainly won't be the last. I'm human. That's what humans do.

This was one of those bad brags that I couldn't spin into a clear positive, except that I got through it. There are so many stories from my life that could be underdog triumph movies: surviving as a "blue baby," meeting and marrying my husband (one day it will be an epic teen romance novel), making it to graduation for my associates degree—and there will be more to come as I grow older.

These stories are epic and important, but my life is more than two or three good, movie-worthy stories, and I don't need to turn every moment of my life into an epic story in order to be worthwhile and brag-worthy.

It's not just about when I won or triumphed. It *is about* what I took from that moment.

There are days, and they will come again, when it doesn't work out. When I'm feeling crummy, when I don't like anything, anyone, or anywhere. When the funk wins. When I'm ill or unprepared. When it doesn't feel like it'll ever work out. And because I want to live an unedited life, I get to brag about those days along with my good and goofy ones. You do, too.

You are allowed to brag about the little nugget of wisdom you dug *deep* to find in your crummy situation. You are allowed to brag about making it through the day (and that's it!).

Brags that claim the hard time and the smallest moment of wisdom are some of the most powerful. They truly encapsulate the side of our lives we often have to keep hidden. It's not required, but when you are able to say, "I lost a client contract today and I realized I'm *relieved* (didn't expect *that*), even though it's a massive financial strain," you access a new level of insight into your own life and the community at large does, too.

Bearing Witness

Another fabulous way of getting used to this practice is learning how to celebrate others and bear witness to their experience. By mastering bearing witness for others, we're also helping to destroy the notion that brags have any sort of hierarchy.

Learning how to bear witness is a gift to everyone in your life. Women, especially, are socialized, expected, and trained to share the burden. Men are socialized to fix things.

What a burden to carry—responsibility for how other people move through the world. Instead, by bearing witness we are able to see how other people are experiencing the world, without the burden. We get to share in their brags instead. We are allowed to celebrate *with them*, even if their brag is hard on them or hard to read or hear about.

The deeper into #BragOutLoud you get, the safer you feel to share your unedited life. Seeing someone's unedited life laid out in front of us can trigger all those messages: "step in, fix, carry the burden."

I am a born fixer. When someone brags about their new porch swing, I want to jump in with "I can help you put it up or repaint the old one!" When I see someone grieving, I want to take away that pain with a corny joke and a casserole. Painting swings and making casseroles is noble, as long as it's not born out of obligation, but my fixer instinct is more often motivated by guilt that I should be doing "more."

Instead of jumping into fixer mode, I have the opportunity with #BragOutLoud to see them as whole and complete in that moment, without my "help." I allow that person to experience the situation completely, without someone else's interference. They get to share without editing or managing my help.

As the head of the #BragOutLoud community, I witness a lot. It can be really, *really, really* hard to sit in that witnessing position, because there aren't words for it. In a text-based community, how do you bear witness without fixing? Without saying something that will make it worse?

It requires a strength I am still developing, but there are some excellent trailblazers in the community that use phrases like, "I see you." "Holding you." "♥" "Taking a deep breath with you." when they want to acknowledge and show support for others' hard or bad days. To bear witness to the struggle.

What a gift, to bear witness or be seen in that way: as complete; as worthy of being seen without fixing. What a beautiful way to experience the massive range of human experiences and celebrate them all, without ranking them, without making these experiences more or less than they are. What a skill to have—to bear witness. What a gift—to be seen.

Being Witnessed

It's healing to say, "My #BragOutLoud is I survived today. That's all I've got in me." To claim such honesty is powerful. Knowing that your brag won't be measured against the scale of worthiness is freeing. Knowing it won't be judged against yesterday's good brag or tomorrow's small victory, that it is still valid. It still counts. To be witnessed is also paramount.

The more we claim these imperfect moments, brag about the crummy, the more permission we give ourselves and others to be fully human: human without editing, without the strain of perfection looming. Just. Human.

Without these bad brags, we're cutting ourselves off before we get going. We *need* the full breadth of experiences. We need the "I won!" *and* the "I struggled/am struggling."

It can be uncomfortable or feel totally new to share a good day or a bad day and have someone witness it and walk away. To be witnessed and stand in that witnessed space allows us to feel the power of bearing witness from the other side. To welcome and trust the acceptance of others.

Accepting the kudos, the "standing with you" and "♥" after a #BragOutLoud is a completely new level of self-compassion and grace pointed inwards. It is an opportunity to allow others to refuel us as we refuel ourselves, as we step into this new world we're creating; to allow a spark of joy to reach us that has no strings, no expectations, no obligations. Joy that is freely given and shared.

Often, it feels easier to brag on the good stuff or to take a minor good thing and find deeper joy or meaning in it. I want to be explicit in our goal to claim *all* the aspects of our experience. So please, brag on the good too. Do whatever's easiest for you in the moment and know that we are safe to share the crummy days too.

We *need* to see that we're more than positive sound bites, that others struggle too. Sometimes they struggle just like us, sometimes not. Without the bad brags, we'll fizzle out. If we're only sharing the good, we're censoring ourselves—which isn't what we're about here. We're trying to live unedited lives with more opportunities for tiny joys.

Sometimes joy lies beyond admitting defeat or our worst days. Sometimes joy is being seen or seeing that someone is in the trenches with us.

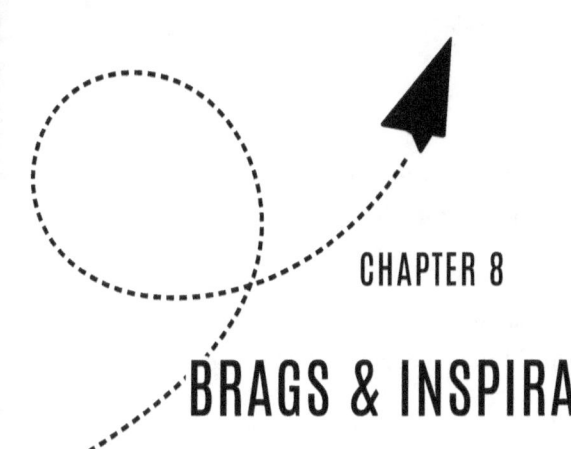

CHAPTER 8

BRAGS & INSPIRATION

Now it's time to start putting these #BragOutLoud moments together, to see how it all works. Below are a handful of examples from community members. You'll see some are straightforward, some are heartfelt, and some have a deeper meaning and impact.

All of them, however, are worthy. There is no hierarchy in #BragOutLoud and, as you'll see, it's life-changing. It's freeing knowing that you can brag about mundane things, life-altering decisions, great struggles, brilliant triumphs, and everything in between without having to edit or worry.

These brags (and celebration examples, which we'll dive into in the next chapters) are here to light the way, spark your imagination, and illustrate how easy it can be.

I had my final live observation, for my certification in my specialty, this week and I passed with flying colors!! I am now officially certified and can charge for offering my services!

Lil' tiny brag. I put a contract in on a property. My dream is to turn it into an all-time inclusive STEM preschool. Scary!

#BragOutLoud—after seven hours of sleep over two days to make all the food, my parents' party was a success! I am so proud that I planned and created tables and tables of food (with help)!

- # I had my first appointment with a new therapist this week and went to the doc for a follow-up appointment. #selfcareissexy

- # I have been really listening to my body this week and practicing self-care!! I took a nap and took things easy.

- # #BragOutLoud I negotiated my business insurance down by 25 percent today! Savings of over $4000 per year!

- # I nurtured this life [the post included planters full of recently bloomed flowers]. In my head I frequently view myself as an impulsive person, but this is proof that I can create a nourishing foundation for anything to grow.

- # Proved that I am not a helicopter mom and that my daughter did indeed have [condition that interferes with her ability to learn] when all of the teachers and doctors first said that she did not. I knew something was going on with her and had her tested two years ago. Last week she did an updated aptitude test and she went up over 26 points and is reading way above grade level now. So I am so glad that I listened to my mom intuition that something was going on with her and got her the proper help.

- # I'm feeling down today and so I've been struggling to think up a brag. So here are some small things:
    - I took my kids to their first day of school.
    - I set up my classroom more.
    - I answered a phone call.
    - I made dinner.
    - I took care of my sick kid.
    - I colored.

\# I am co-authoring a book with some other amazing ladies and today I found out my chapter is going to be the first. The feelings involved with this are crazy—I am of course excited and feeling like, "Wow!! I will be the first chapter people read." Then I am like, "Oh no, I will be the first chapter people read. What if it's not good enough? What if it doesn't hold everyone's interest so they stop reading, then everyone else's chapters won't be read?" Then I go back to, "Well, they know what they are doing, and they must have liked mine enough to put it first." Sorry for writing a book to explain my thoughts. It's a whirlwind.

\# I have not posted much. I have family in town and I *just opened escrow on a house.* #BragOutLoud Thanks for allowing me to sneak in and out of this group :)

\# My brag was definitely dancing until my legs gave out at my best friend's wedding!!

\# I'm not very green-fingered. I've been longing for a flower bed since we moved into this house three years ago. My hubby gave me "that look." Seriously, I'm the girl that can kill a cactus. Anyway, last month I decided to get a gardener in to put in a flower bed. And it's growing!! I've got roses and hydrangeas and gladiolus and sunflowers! #BragOutLoud

\# So … *loads* to brag about; however, I'm going to put my big girl pants on and brag that I found out over the weekend that I'm "officially" a millionaire. One of my investments is now worth a million bucks. #BragOutLoud

\# I've forgotten to brag, and some days didn't feel like I had much to brag about. Bragging about that because I didn't beat myself up over it. I'm learning to use better language when I don't do something as well as I feel I should, so this is a pretty big deal!

\# This may seem little; however, I was able to get all of our laundry washed, folded, and put away!! #BragOutLoud

\# I shared this with my private group and was totally freaking out to brag about it here. Then I was like "Heck, there was a time when I had zero bucks, so I'm *bragging* baby! *Wooo weeee!*" [attached to this brag was an image of multiple PayPal payment notifications via email]

\# Bragging that my kids are returning in two days after being away for a month, the house isn't ready for their return, and I'm totally *not* freaking out! Bragging that I decided we'll make it a fun group project to paint and get their rooms set up, together! :) #BragOutLoud

\# I got a job and start next week! #BragOutLoud

\# So, my #BragOutLoud moment: I used the hell out of my kitchen today, making three different meals (enough for five to seven servings each), and freezing the last of my coffee for iced coffee.

\# This kind of relates to my brag from yesterday. But today I avoided reaching out to many of the toxic people that I decided to avoid yesterday. I have a really hard time with unresolved endings. So I tend to continue to talk to people that I know I should be finished with. But I didn't today. And I ended up in a much more emotionally healthy place at the end of the day. #BragOutLoud

\# I'm gonna #BragOutLoud about the taboo *nap I took*! I

wanted it, I needed it, I deserved it, I did nothing to "earn" it. Still deserved it.

This coffee was free from the car in front of me! It's so weird to brag about something I didn't "earn."

My big brag is that I've lost 25 lbs. in the last four months! I started a new lifestyle to be healthier, not to lose weight, but the weight loss is an encouraging side effect! My #BragOutLoud today is that I bought pants that fit my new waist!

Today is a *huge* #BragOutLoud for me. This morning, as I walked past the mirror, post-workout, sweaty, messy hair, and red-faced, the first thought that came to my mind was "Dang, I am beautiful!" It wasn't just a thought, it was a feeling that I felt deep in my heart, filling it, and I truly felt happy, complete, and fulfilled. The thing is, it wasn't just saying this to myself, but it was actually believing what I said. I believed what I said because I felt it in my heart—that was a *huge* deal for me.

#BragOutLoud—I let myself use my support system today. I leaned on my friends. I vented without guilt—okay—with *much* less guilt. I let them love and see for me, since I couldn't for myself. Then—*then* I believed them, because they are safe. I took care, I took a nap, I watched a silly movie. I straightened up the house.

#BragOutLoud—I made a phone call. I hate talking on the phone, but it's done!

I know my inner voice is telling me I'm not supposed to brag about intimate things, but I was at a conference all weekend and on the drive back I snuck in a stop with my husband. All

we did was make out like two teenagers on his lunch break, but it was so fun. Who does that? I felt so giddy on the way home—totally worth it!

\# I decided to sign up to volunteer several months ago just to have the experience. I'm placing goals for myself on the road ahead so that I can actually *do* the things I always think "I wish I could" or "I really should do that some time"—I'm actually going to *do* those things. One goal at a time. You have to take one step to take another. I met new people and enjoyed myself. Most importantly—I was aware. I was in control. I was capable. It was empowering and felt fantastic. #BragOutLoud

The examples on the last several pages are just the start; on the next page you've got an inspiration list of free brags—situations and examples of things you can brag about that don't require you to change the world. The great thing about brags is: Even if you haven't done the brag, you can pick from the list, do it, and brag about it.

Many times, we find ourselves spinning on what to brag about *or* not feeling like we have anything we can brag about. Not anymore! Close your eyes and pick, choose a random number between one and 100, or scan the list and see what feels the easiest to do.

Then do it. Now, claim it as your #BragOutLoud. Celebrate afterwards.

Scribble on these pages, add in your own examples. Cross out the ones that you hate. Ask your friends what they would add.

#BragOutLoud Inspiration

1. Putting clean sheets on the bed.
2. Tossing out old food.
3. Taking a shower.
4. Throwing away old cosmetics/lotion/perfume.
5. Taking a walk.
6. Refilling your water.
7. Eating a meal.
8. Grabbing a snack.
9. Looking for a brag on this list.
10. Posting your #BragOutLoud moment.
11. Sharing your biggest accomplishment ever.
12. Telling us your last charitable act/donation.
13. Sharing your most recent healthy choice.
14. Indulging in your latest guilty pleasure.
15. Saying yes to that inner voice.
16. Putting on clean underwear.
17. Using your blinker.
18. Going grocery shopping.
19. Savoring your favorite treat.
20. Going for a walk/run/class/movement thingy.
21. Finishing that last book.
22. Showing up today.
23. Smiling.
24. Taking a break.
25. Getting 'it' done.
26. Finishing that season on Netflix.
27. Asking for help.
28. Taking your supplements/meds/vitamins.
29. Putting on music to work by.
30. Staying warm/cool.
31. Sending love out into the universe.
32. Waking up today.
33. Starting that project you've been avoiding.
34. Getting out of the house.
35. Snuggling up.
36. Closing your eyes and recuperating for three minutes.
37. Looking for answers.
38. Caring about anything—ever.
39. Putting something away.
40. Working on your self-talk.
41. Trying to love yourself more.
42. Wanting more for yourself and others.
43. Trying something new.
44. Getting gas/refilling your metro card.
45. Eating yummy food.
46. Setting that goal.
47. Working towards your goals.
48. Stumbling.
49. Trying.
50. Loving.

51. Ordering/asking for what you need.
52. Trying to meditate.
53. Attempting self-care.
54. Looking for something beautiful.
55. Getting the mail.
56. Loving on an animal.
57. Working.
58. Resting.
59. Using the fancy stationery.
60. Landing that gig.
61. Saying no.
62. Trying to socialize.
63. Looking up at the sky.
64. Enjoying the rain.
65. Talking with a friend.
66. Finding a penny.
67. Turning in your reward points.
68. Using a gift card.
69. Saying yes when it felt good.
70. Upsizing your movie popcorn.
71. Drinking water.
72. Brushing your teeth.
73. Swapping out the laundry.
74. Swaying to the music.
75. Cleaning off your workspace.
76. Trying a new recipe.
77. Returning a library book.
78. Opening the windows for a breeze.
79. Lighting the candle you've been saving.
80. Turning your phone off for 30 minutes.
81. Starting your grocery list.
82. Putting on your favorite scent.
83. Looking through old photos.
84. Washing your face.
85. Sitting outside with a fresh tea/coffee.
86. Writing in your journal.
87. Stretching your arms.
88. Reading your favorite book.
89. Closing your laptop.
90. Turning off your notifications.
91. Trying to setup a girls' date.
92. Sneaking some wildflowers into the house.
93. Doodling in the margins.
94. Sending a thank you card.
95. Recycling anything.
96. Swapping out your seasonal clothes.
97. Ordering takeout instead of cooking.
98. Watering the plants.
99. Putting on some lotion.
100. Taking a deeeeeep breath.

And if that's a little too overwhelming, you can go to BragOutLoud Book.com/Inspiration and download the "What Can I #BragOutLoud About gif" and it will choose for you! There will be updated lists, gifs, and inspiration in the same place—so check it out, get inspired, and start percolating your first #BragOutLoud!

CHAPTER 9

WHAT DOES CELEBRATION MEAN?

The second part of #BragOutLoud is the celebration. Celebration in our new world is defined as: a pause and intentional expansion into joy.

The pause is key. It's non-negotiable.

There are hundreds of reasons why we're still searching for the right tool to keep up with life, to combat the bone-weary tiredness we struggle with. Hundreds of reasons why we're burned out in so many areas of our lives.

The brag, that recognition, is critical. But without the pause, we're sabotaging our own hard work. If we don't start pausing, we cannot fully appreciate everything that makes up our lives. It's hard to brag about that new sponge, if we don't pause and really *feel* the tiny spark of joy it gives us.

Ultimately, regardless of the brag *or* the form of celebration, we're exploring ways to expand into more joy. More joy is the goal, because with more joy, we have more patience and more compassion for ourselves and others, and we'll experience fewer burnout symptoms.

How we celebrate is just as varied as the brags we recognize. There is no right or wrong way to celebrate.

Deserving a Celebration

We've been socialized to think of celebrations in a fairly specific context. We've learned to celebrate the events that *warrant a celebration*. But what does that really mean? We celebrate the obvious things: birthdays, anniversaries, sporting events, marriages, births, graduations, memorials, holidays, etc. Yay!

However, these occasions come with a lot of cultural expectations: size, cost, effort, etc. We learn to use these situations as an outlet for joy. We have parties for things that *deserve it*. This leaves a *substantial* gap in our lives: What about our small victories, what about the secret triumphs, what about the battles no one sees?

Celebration in the #BragOutLoud movement aims to give breathing room for all those unsung moments—all of those things we don't throw parties for. Unfortunately, we've been socialized to believe that if we celebrate too much, we'll devalue the "big" events.

I can understand how, on the surface, that feels right. But I'm here to tell you, these big events wear us out because not only are they generally a lot of work, but we aren't used to feeling that much joy.

Joy isn't meant to be portioned out in small doses. We've learned to reserve joy, put it on a shelf, and only take it down when it's the right time. Which means we're not used to joy.

We experience this sort of joy whiplash. We wear ourselves out trying to contain all the joy we might feel on our birthdays, at a wedding, or when we accomplish a lifelong goal. Afterwards, we need a longer refueling period *or* we hold back on experiencing joy, fearing it will be taken away from us. We fall into the trap of "foreboding joy," as Brené Brown calls it.

The radical solution is to experience joy more often, in small and intentional bursts, so we can get used to it, so that we can hold even greater reserves of joy with us for all of those big events and simpler events in our lives.

And as we build our endurance for holding joy, we get to be happier, healthier, and more satisfied.

Keep it Simple

How do you celebrate, then? Make it easy.

The simpler the celebration, the easier it is to do and incorporate into your daily life. We're going for a good feeling, an extended moment of satisfaction or joy. As long as you're intentional about claiming your celebration, anything can be a celebration.

Make it as easy as you possibly can. You could dance, you could listen to your favorite song, you could refill your water, you could literally smell the roses. Label that as your celebration and you've celebrated.

You are taking a moment to feel as good as you can about what you just recognized. (There will be a whole list of ways to celebrate in the following chapters, just like we had for brags.)

We're normalizing an incredible exercise in self-care. We are using celebration as a way to change our internal dialogue. That internal culture we've been developing our whole lives is evolving as we claim our celebrations as restorative moments.

We are also modeling for everyone around us how simple it could be. Imagine if your coworkers took a break, stood up, did a little shimmy, and felt *really good* for an extra 30 seconds a day. Can you see how quickly that could spread, how seeing someone get up and do their celebration could inspire you to do the same? The change is so minor and the effort so comparatively small for exponential results: more spots of joy throughout the day.

Normalizing Celebration

Normalizing celebration and joy outside of those big events is just one of the many benefits of reclaiming celebration as part of our #BragOutLoud movement. Of course, when we start to discuss celebrating when we "haven't done anything to deserve it," we hit a roadblock.

We've been socialized, especially as women, to avoid anything that makes us stick out. We might be labeled a show-off. No one wants that. If we're labeled a show-off, that means we didn't really earn the right to celebrate or claim what we did. We're politely or snidely being called liars.

Eww.

The core of that slight is really about triggering someone else and what they've unquestioningly labeled as acceptable behaviors. By acting outside of what they think is appropriate, we appear frivolous, or our joy might make them feel bad.

We don't want our coworkers, our friends, or loved ones to feel jealous or hurt because we celebrated with an extra treat or public declaration. Not everyone can celebrate with a spa day or a treat and our fear of claiming that publicly can hold us back.

Which is exactly why we need to start sharing our #BragOutLoud and celebrations. Because when the brags don't have a hierarchy, when anything can be a celebration, we can finally start to share our joy with others, without editing.

Just because you can celebrate with a new pair of shoes doesn't mean your celebration was more worthwhile than my celebratory cup of coffee at home. What's important is that we both chose to pause, kindling that little spark of joy.

We can finally take the sting of competition, hurt, jealousy, or lack out of our joy and fully express it. Sharing our joy over the small, the big, and the mundane without worrying how it will be received is a game changer. Dropping the worry gives us more energy.

Now my celebration and your celebration can focus on feeling good—instead of worrying if we've satisfied that external scale of what we're allowed to say, feel, or experience. We begin to shift into our unedited lives, with more joy, more satisfaction, and a band of women in our lives doing the same.

CHAPTER 10

DANCING IN THE KITCHEN

Mastering celebration doesn't require the perfect outfit and 10 fewer pounds or expensive rituals, parties, etc. It's all about the pause, the prioritization of self.

Instead of stressing about doing it right, start small and simple. Treat yourself to a treat already stashed in your home. Do you have a bottle of sparkling cider or wine hidden in the back of a cupboard? Could you make your favorite meal? How about diving into the last season of your favorite comedy?

What feels restorative to you? Is it a moment of quiet? A good workout? What about a meal with friends or loved ones?

Take an inventory for yourself. When do you feel the most satisfied? When do you feel the most yourself? What gives you a burst of energy and a goofy smile?

Any and all of those things can be a celebration.

Feeling More Deeply

For me, it's dancing in the kitchen. I feel goofy, but the movement is freeing and the grin that crops up can't be stopped. I don't have to dance specific moves or go for hours. Thirty seconds of jumping, spinning, and rocking my hips makes me feel awake, loved, inspired, and satisfied.

Having a go-to celebration that doesn't require any cash, time, resources, or preparation is vital for myself and most of the community. The act of prioritizing *how I feel as I pause and expand into joy* truly is radical.

It is a declaration of my priorities. It's an acknowledgement that I am worth being my own top priority.

My silly celebration, dancing in the kitchen, doesn't take away from anyone I love and care about. In fact, it adds to my reserves. It creates a calm and peace that allows me to more fully show up for everyone around me.

When I dance in the kitchen, I feel more energized. I remember how much I love it, how good I feel afterwards, how much more I have to brag about.

I'd love to throw a party every time I accomplish a big goal or land a contract or travel or speak or meet a new friend or make the perfect cup of coffee, but that's not always possible. The more I celebrate and brag, the more those tiny moments give me the same thrill as a well-hosted and enjoyed party.

But, it's not about the party. It's about the feeling. It's about the ability to feel more deeply.

Celebrating on the Bad Days

This ability to feel more deeply is even more necessary when our brags are about the crumminess of certain days. Our celebrations are even more critical when our brags are: "I made it out of bed today.

No shower, no motivation, but I made it to the living room." On those days, the kitchen dance becomes a wiggle on the couch.

Sometimes celebrating is letting it all out and having a good cry, or a fourth cup of coffee, or a nap. But it counts. It has to.

There is no hierarchy. There is only the chance to feel joy or feel better. There is only the devotion to our own self-worth.

You deserve whatever celebration you can manage. Even when we get caught celebrating, which can be awkward, it's still worth it. That's why we have a community where we share.

A community of courageous people who are celebrating by hiding from their precious kiddos in the bathroom for three minutes or by picking up a pizza on the way home or scheduling a doctor's appointment. Or dancing in their kitchen.

We come back to the community to normalize this process so that when we're caught celebrating and it doesn't make sense to the people who catch us, we still feel safe and secure. We know that the process may appear different, but that the rewards are exponential. We come back to the community when we feel a bit embarrassed for getting caught dancing in the kitchen or bragging about a new trash can. We dance in the kitchen anyway.

We try. We forget. We try again. We allow ourselves to start unpacking why we feel obligated to edit our lives. We realize we're not alone. We celebrate as much, as often, and as deeply as we can. You have the permission to try.

My goal is for you to now be able to find your brag and plan your celebration in as little as 90 seconds. Maybe you'll need five minutes for your celebration, or a whole week. Maybe you'll only need 30 seconds to dance like a wild woman. Regardless, refueling is what makes celebration worthwhile.

You deserve those 30 seconds of celebration to refuel.

CHAPTER 11

CELEBRATIONS & INSPIRATION

Now it's on to the *fun part*—celebrations!! Again, here are a few examples from the #BragOutLoud community. I encourage you to cultivate your very own short list of go-to celebrations.

Celebrated by digging into the cleaning I had been procrastinating on previously!

I responded with heartfelt compassion and stood up for myself when someone lashed out at me unexpectedly. I told two people I was proud of myself as the celebration.

Celebrated by taking my partner out for drinks and street tacos—yum.

Watermelon wheat ale brewed here at Potrero Beach!

Oooh—had not thought of a celebration. I will do a little dance once I can be bothered to get out of bed—or maybe staying in bed can be the celebration!!

Tonight, I celebrated by high fiving my partner!

Celebration: apple fritter and coffee.

My closing was yesterday, and I followed your advice, Shannon! I had a massage this morning and it was wonderful!

Used those frozen coffee cubes to make a frappe of sorts and it was soooooooo good.

Decided to take my husband away on a training weekend I had already booked on the 22nd so that we can steal a bit of abundant loving time together!!

I celebrated by just letting it sink in. I am healthier, I'm making better choices, and I feel better about myself!

Celebrating by looking in the mirror and telling myself "I got this!"

I'm off to buy two ice creams to celebrate with hubby when he gets home.

I am celebrating by watching a yule fire on YouTube and allowing memories from my childhood to flood my soul in celebration of loved ones gone before me.

I splurged on insurmountable levels of vegan food and booked time to pet cats at an animal rescue on the way home.

How did I celebrate? I allowed myself to be washed over by feelings of self-love.

Celebrated with a long bath this evening—after far too long sweating over the laptop.

I'm celebrating by taking a stretch this morning to thank my body for walking and biking so much.

I did my butt and core practice then meditated and realized the opportunity I got was a gift for *me* to let myself open. It was a crazy amazing meditation!

- \# I'm celebrating being productive in the kitchen by being in bed with my giant bowl of salad and binging on TV. Just owning the veg-out status like #BragOutLoud says it's OK to do.

- \# I celebrated by hiding in the bathroom, door locked, to get five minutes to myself. I felt so refreshed!

- \# Sleep?? Yeah, I'm going to sleep as celebration—the wedding has been fun *and* hectic. Sleep sounds so good to me right now.

- \# I am celebrating by wearing a hoodie. What is special about this hoodie? I bought it in Vegas last November and it shrunk in the wash. It didn't fit well, and it is snug now but fits better so I am wearing it to celebrate getting stronger every day.

- \# I came home and watched a good movie.

- \# I snuggled in the hammock with a good book for two whole hours—the kids knew it was my celebration time and they loved it. They brought me snacks!

Allow this list to evolve over time, change with the seasons, have different feelings and intensities. Regardless of the celebration, it all counts. Remember, it's about the pause and intentional expansion into joy. No qualifiers. No secret checklist or obligations.

So, if angry music feels like a spark of joy—rock it out. If a quiet moment under a tree feels restorative—do it. You officially have permission to celebrate in any way that feels good to *you*.

Next are 100 ways you can celebrate that don't cost a thing and can be done in no time. This is not a definitive or even exhaustive list. These ideas are a jumping-off point; hopefully a source of inspiration.

Edit this list—mark off the ones you hate, tweak them to fit your abilities and preferences. Create your shortlist on the empty page, snap a picture, and use it as your phone background.

#Celebrate Inspiration

1. Refill your water.
2. Dance for 30 seconds.
3. Use your gift cards.
4. Use that spice mix you've been saving.
5. Read a chapter of your favorite book.
6. Go for a walk.
7. Play with your favorite animals.
8. Check the mail.
9. Paint your fingers/toes.
10. Journal.
11. Meditate.
12. Find your favorite song and jam out.
13. Dance in the kitchen.
14. Try a new recipe with items you already have.
15. Eat an apple.
16. Make backyard s'mores.
17. Sit outside and enjoy the bats at twilight.
18. Look up at the stars/moon/clouds.
19. Earthing/grounding.
20. Go for a drive.
21. Watch the clouds move by.
22. Catch the sunset.
23. Stretch your body.
24. Lay on the floor and look at the ceiling/fan.
25. Dress up.
26. Wear the fancy jewelry.
27. Try a new hairdo.
28. Snuggle with your puppy/kitty/anyone's baby.
29. Straighten up.
30. Do the dishes.
31. Start your grocery list.
32. Call a friend.
33. Post pictures you "never had time for."
34. Send a love note.
35. Put on lipstick.
36. Brush your hair.
37. Reach out and connect with intention.
38. Share an intimate moment with a partner.
39. Listen to a podcast.
40. Watch a video or a movie.
41. Use your art supplies.
42. Set a date for your hobby.
43. Color in your coloring book.
44. Shut your laptop for 15 minutes.
45. Bask.
46. Post your #BragOutLoud.
47. Literally pat yourself on the back.
48. Go pee.
49. Wash your face.
50. Change your underwear right now.

51. Set a "binge date."
52. Water your plants.
53. Put on that scarf with a flourish.
54. Freshen your tea.
55. Grab a salty snack.
56. Use your favorite pen to write, "I love you."
57. Soak your feet in a warm bath.
58. Daydream.
59. Plan a half-day adventure.
60. Throw away an old pair of underwear.
61. Wear your fuzzy socks.
62. Open the curtains and smile.
63. Put on lotion.
64. Take a nap.
65. Karate chop the air like a ninja.
66. Watch something that makes you laugh.
67. Relive your happiest memory and bask.
68. Make "bad" art.
69. Take a shower.
70. Use your favorite mug.
71. Change your sheets.
72. Set your phone down and walk away.
73. Close your eyes for three minutes.
74. Use the fancy bath products.
75. Find a flower and smell it.
76. Use the fancy stationery.
77. Make a cup of coffee.
78. Clean off your workspace.
79. Open a window.
80. Light a candle.
81. Doodle.
82. Use a heating pad and warm up.
83. Turn the fan on and cool off.
84. Read a saved article on your phone.
85. Strike a pose in the mirror and giggle.
86. Go for a run.
87. Listen to your favorite song.
88. Sing along to a musical.
89. Schedule a friend date.
90. Clear off an afternoon of obligations.
91. Sip a smoothie.
92. Do five minutes of yoga.
93. Air guitar (or drum solo) all by yourself.
94. Use that freebie you snatched.
95. Indulge your sweet tooth.
96. Create a new playlist.
97. Go to the gym.
98. Take a selfie.
99. Jump on the bed.
100. Breathe.

And to simplify it all, you can go to BragOutLoudBook.com/Inspiration and download the "How Can I #Celebrate gif" and it will choose for you! There will be updated lists, gifs, and inspiration in the same place—so check it out, get inspired, and start percolating your first celebration!

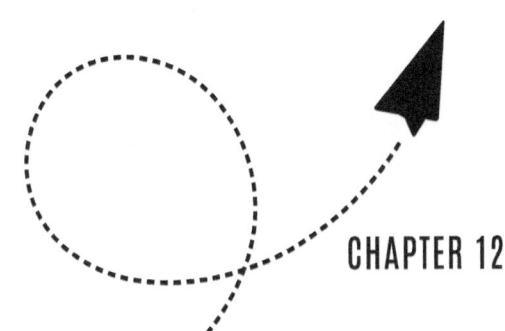

CHAPTER 12

WHAT IF I DON'T HAVE A BRAG?

You've got the basics. I promise. The more you practice, the better you'll get. You are officially granted permission to stumble, practice, not feel perfect, and feel the twinge of unease as you go.

But then, what do you do if you don't have a brag? If you've racked your brain, hated the inspiration from the previous chapters, and you're still one giant blank? What do you do then? There are several options to pull you out of this *very natural, very common* experience of feeling uncertain about bragging. We all land here, frequently.

Here are eight different ways you can brag. Think of them as sandboxes to play in.

A Blast from the Past

Look back at your past and search for something you've never bragged about before. There are *plenty of times* in our lives where we couldn't fully process, experience, or be giddy over something. Sometimes it's because we didn't have the time. Or we didn't feel safe. Or it was big and special to us, but the rest of the world didn't think so.

This is my favorite example (it's mine):

> I got the lead in a play as a junior. It was **so much fun**, but I never felt like I could really enjoy it fully, since it was such a small production and some of my friends didn't get parts. Today I celebrated by playing out my favorite moments while I sipped on a fresh coffee. (I wish it'd been a musical, because then I could jam to the soundtrack!)

Just because this happened 15 years ago doesn't diminish its impact. When I walked in to the school, there was a throng of students with a lot of mingled emotions: excitement for me, disappointment for themselves, and jealousy. So I tried to keep as much of what I was feeling inside as I could. I didn't want to hurt anyone's feelings, so I kept silent—even though I knew it was going to be a huge undertaking and all I wanted to do was scream from the rooftops with pride.

You don't have to use anything this "big" for yours, it just needs to spark something for *you*. Others in the community have used breakups, first cars, honor rolls, daring adventures, vacations, and small life decisions to brag on. The point is to find and expand your joy—which has no time limit. Now, scribble a couple of past brags you can use in the future in the space on the next page.

WHAT IF I DON'T HAVE A BRAG? 83

#BragOutLouds from your past:

Eyeing the Future

Scan the future for something you are looking forward to and share about it. You are allowed to preemptively brag about things in your life, to celebrate them in advance. I love this approach because it helps lessen your likelihood to put off or hold back and only brag when some future *big, big* goal is completely finished.

Instead, you're taking a little piece of that future event and granting it its own joy, its own space. I promise it won't diminish the future event's joyfulness. An easy example we see more and more is when people share about their upcoming vacations. It's lovely to #BragOutLoud and celebrate plane tickets—you should. I also think we should be bragging about all the prep work it takes to go on vacation. Why not brag about narrowing down which miniature golf courses you're going to visit in Kalamazoo? How lovely it is to celebrate with a hot cup of tea after digging the luggage out of the basement!

There's no reason to limit ourselves, so if there are a few things on the horizon for you—it's time to brag about the small steps you're taking to get there.

#BragOutLouds from your future:

Brag. Repeat. Brag. Repeat.

Brag on repeat. You are allowed to brag about the same thing as many times as you'd like.

Brag every day about your workout success, making the bed, getting to work on time, finding a parking spot, or not screaming at loved ones.

It all counts. The rest of the world may hate hearing about your daily rituals, but that's because they're not used to being in a community like ours. Most of us have felt the guilty pang of "Oh, I should already be good at this *normal, adult daily habit*" when seeing spotless bathrooms in selfies or sweaty workout pics. It happens to all of us, but here—in the #BragOutLoud community—there's no guilt. Just space. Space to recognize whatever small step you're taking and then celebrate the heck out of it.

Take some time and use the space on the next page to jot down the things you already do and don't take the time to recognize. Maybe it's using moisturizer, taking your vitamins, making the bed, getting in your workout, or snuggling up to read before bed.

#BragOutLoud on repeat ideas:

Trying is Enough

Brag about looking for a brag. This may sound silly, but the fact that you are sitting down, committed to trying, is worth bragging about.

What this really comes down to is recognizing your effort in general. Taking the time to *try* is sorely underrated in our culture. We're simply not taught to value the preparation time until *after* the goal is achieved. Once the goal is achieved, we can honor the time, effort, and energy it took to succeed, but not before.

We very much put that notion on its head here. We are doing a process, a practice. Pausing and honoring that process and doing so *while it is happening* is vital.

This is also a good time to look at the things we typically frame as being crummy. I know that, personally, when I'm struggling the most to find a brag, it's because I had a bad day. A day that wouldn't rank in the top million bad days on the planet, but really wasn't fun for me. They're the days where not-ideal problems crop up, all day long.

Those are the worst, and when I struggle the hardest. If it's a genuinely bad day, I can look for the silver lining, the deeper message. But when it's just a crummy day, all I want to do is grumble. On those days, it's easiest to claim the fact that I tried and move on.

On more than one occasion, on these days, all I've managed to write is, "Today, my #BragOutLoud is I looked for one and nothing felt right. I tried. That counts, and I'll be celebrating with a glass of water."

#BragOutLoud for trying ideas:

Taboo Brags: Sex, Money, Religion, Boasting, and Other "No-Nos"

Find a new category to brag in. It might be time to stretch out into uncharted territory.

Things we can check off from a to-do list make for great #BragOutLoud moments, but sometimes that doesn't feel right or exciting enough. When you finally reach that point, then, it's time to look at an area you might not have considered before.

Since there is no hierarchy to brags, it means that nothing is really off-limits, including taboo topics. This obviously doesn't mean I'm okay with bragging about cruelty or malicious activity. You know that, and it must be said for legal reasons. With nothing off-limits, we approach this category with heightened awareness and care.

Most of us also carry around a list of taboo subjects; subjects we don't talk about out of comfort, respect, or politeness.

I understand—*and I challenge these assumptions.* If the community you're sharing with is safe, and if your intent in the sharing is one of personal growth (as opposed to shaming, putting someone in their place, or personal gain/coercion)—we should be able to share without harm.

That's not to say it won't be a challenge sometimes! However, when we begin to frame our taboo brags as opportunities for deep appreciation and freedom, it can be magical.

Sex becomes intimacy; which can include everything from shared intimacy and connection with a partner, a touching moment with your chosen family, or the healing touch of therapy.

Money becomes finances; which can include unexpected windfalls, a shiny penny you found, a discount you snagged, or how your investments are faring.

Religion becomes faith; the small ways you feel affirmed, the good deeds of your faith-based organization, fellowship of your place of worship, or the freedom you feel in worship.

Boasting becomes selflessness; how you prioritize charitable giving, the benefits you gain when you give up your seat at the table, how you recognized and mitigated your privilege, or how you chose to pick trash up from the parking lot.

*Politics becomes shared goals**; focusing on volunteering to support your local community, voting in the school board elections, or helping your niece with her student government posters.

*Your focus is on the way you feel inspired, not the issues at hand (safe space for all, remember).

Mental health becomes self-compassion; going to therapy/counseling, investing in a new journal, combating your inner critic with facts of your awesomeness, self-directed grace, or a nap.

This is obviously not an exhaustive list, but it is a beginning for you to start brainstorming all those little things you keep locked away or unsaid because as a kid you learned, "We don't talk about that." Here, when we talk about it with integrity, grace, and intention—we begin the healing process of claiming all parts of us!

#BragOutLouds on taboo subjects:

Vulnerability Versus Shame

Brag about the thing you were shamed for. This can be challenging; shame is a powerful bodily experience.

However, when we take the time to explore (in a safe environment) the things we felt shame or embarrassment over, we can heal in unexpected ways. Shame, guilt, and embarrassment are often used interchangeably, but are vastly different—look at the work of Brené Brown for a powerful examination of shame and vulnerability. I'll be using *embarrassment* to cover a wide range of experiences.

Embarrassment is a big thing to tackle and should be done in a safe place. #BragOutLoud should never take the place of quality mental health care. Full stop.

And we can use the #BragOutLoud practice to explore the gunk from our past that is not fully founded in reality. There are plenty of situations where, because someone was trying to protect us, we internalized a bit of shame.

Maybe our loud laugh grated on someone's nerves. Now we can begin to release that by bragging about our lovely, raucous laugh.

Perhaps our art supplies added to the mess in the living room, but today we dig them out and set aside the internalized message of "You're messy."

What if your freckles were your least favorite feature? Today you could continue to reclaim their beauty.

Tackling these kinds of brags often has a kind of *expansion whiplash effect*, in that we experience great power, healing, and oftentimes big feelings, and soon after feel the emotional and physical exhaustion. While this can be common, again, I insist that you do so in a safe environment and seek additional support as you need it. You deserve that kind of support, and I give you *full, unequivocal permission* to seek it out and use it.

What if I don't have a brag? 95

#BragOutLouds on old embarrassments:

Find Inspiration

You don't have to figure this out on your own. You can "steal" someone else's inspiration, or you can also to go to www.BragOutLoudBook.com/Inspiration and find some ideas, tools, and handy downloads. Then brag about it!!

This one is my favorite; I use it frequently:

> *Today I couldn't think of anything to quickly #BragOutLoud about, so I used the gif and it told me to brag about staying hydrated! So I drank a glass of water! Celebrated with Halloween candy!*

I also love when community members brag about using these tools, because it inspires others to do the same! There's nothing wrong with leaning on premade brags, celebrations, or inspiration. In fact, it's one of the smartest things you can give yourself permission to do.

There's no need for you to *work for your brags*. We already work our tails off, just making it through the day. Plus, if you spend a ton of time trying to find the perfect brag and celebration combo, you'll never get it done in as little as 90 seconds.

We don't want that. We want the joy, the recognition, the bright spot. You deserve it. So use the tools here, in the book, online, in the community, and with your favorite people.

#BragOutLouds on finding inspiration:

Be Bold: Go Tiny

No hierarchy means: no hierarchy. Brag about the smallest, tiniest thing you can.

After pages and pages of potentially uncomfortable suggestions, I think it's important that the last suggestion be the smallest.

You are allowed to brag about the tiniest of tiny things: not crying over a snag on your sweater, finding a glitter heart on the ground, buying a new sponge, getting five extra minutes of sleep, or finding change in the sofa.

We're socialized to only recognize the big, the bold, the daring. We learn that only the world-changing things are worth mentioning. One of the fastest ways to reprogram this internalized behavior is to look for the opposite. Instead of searching for the big, we boldly claim the tiny. The smallest brags often lead to the biggest growth, because we see that even with the simplest moment, we have access to more potential joy than we ever realized.

The process of bragging and celebrating comes with a lot of cultural baggage, a lot of preconceived notions about what's worthy. In the #BragOutLoud community, all of our brags are worthy, regardless of size, scope, impact, or influence.

Combating that worthiness narrative leads to more joy and safer, more inclusive communities. For myself, and most of the community, this process started to truly take root when we could stop and recognize the smallest moments. The tiniest choices.

Here is your chance to do the same. Be **bold**. Go tiny.

#BragOutLoud micro moments:

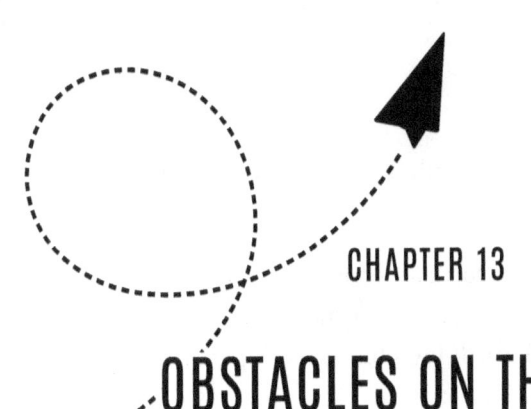

CHAPTER 13

OBSTACLES ON THE PATH

About now, you're probably wrestling with, "How long until it feels normal and doesn't make my belly flip when I brag?"

I wish the answer was concrete. I wish I could say that after 37 genuine #BragOutLoud and celebration combos, you're all set. Ready to move on. Or if you take it as a 30-day challenge, by the end you'll feel like this is "normal."

It truly depends on the individual. For me it took about five weeks, and now most days it feels normal. The deeper I look at my brags or tackle a new kind of brag, the more likely I am to feel that unease. Now I know that feeling means I should, at the very least, sit with the potential brag. I explore what is causing my unease and then decide how much I want to share out loud.

The more you've internalized the common culture, the longer you might need. I hope this comes as a relief. It means the older you are, the more you've been socialized to do the exact opposite of #BragOutLoud. So give yourself some slack. You deserve a bit of extra grace and compassion.

It takes as long as it takes, but the more you do it, the stronger you get. #BragOutLoud is many things, including an endurance game. The more you practice, the easier it will become. It will also be something you might struggle with. I know I still stumble, and I've been consistent for a while now.

Being in our online #BragOutLoud community and actively witnessing the brags of others helps too, so stay engaged. Even if that means you hang out and watch for a bit. Checking in, normalizing bragging and celebrating. It's a journey.

The important part is to keep going. You are likely to forget to do a daily #BragOutLoud. That's okay. That's typical. I forget sometimes as well, and this is my crusade. I've literally set alarms in my calendar and phone, to remind me. That's not cheating—it's setting yourself up for success. Use whatever tool you can think of to support the journey: reminders, alarms, accountability with your friends, or a journal. Put sticky notes on your mirror, refrigerator, and in the pantry. If those stop working, swap them out for something else.

Going Deeper

We've redefined and reclaimed brag. So as long as we're not using it as a weapon (how bragging is traditionally seen), you're okay.

Sometimes you might be faking it, or it feels a bit/very cheesy, because we're really close to a deep truth. If so, try taking a deep breath and examine, "What did this moment *really* give me? What freedom did it give my soul?" Sometimes we find gold in the answer. Our awkwardness dissolves and we're left with a profound sense of "Huh!"

You might just realize that "faking it" and claiming that you distracted yourself from applying for a keynote speaking gig actually felt good. Not having to wait on an answer, not having to negotiate, not having to prepare a video, not having to smash a work event in between your yearly family vacation and anniversary filled you with relief instead of dread or obligation.

Or you might realize, "This is one heck of a pattern I've developed. I guess it's time to get different support to get through it."

There is a gift in bragging often, about small things, or things that feel uneasy. We start to dig deeper and find truths about ourselves and how we're living our lives. We can discover patterns without judgment or harshness. We can address these patterns with grace, patience, and choice if we want to.

Compare and Despair

A common pitfall is comparison. It's alluring to try and make sure your brag compares well with another community member's. It's okay; it can be hard to brag about your new clipboard, when the post before yours is about surviving a funeral.

There is no hierarchy in pain, in brags, in worthiness. Since there is no hierarchy, you have the freedom to share your reality just like everyone else. The beautiful thing I hear over and over again is how good this contrast feels as a community member. I've been told: "I was so scared to share how hard it was to get through the breakup, but knowing I could share without bringing anyone down, and that other people were happy in their own relationships at the same time, weirdly helped."

Which also means that your brags and celebrations don't have to be perfect. I know I've wasted a lot of time trying to find the perfect brag, the perfect way to frame my celebration so it felt worthy. The only way to get over that feeling is through it. But you don't have to do it alone. We're all struggling with the perfection gremlins, so just try.

There's no other way to get the hang of it, than to practice. To see others doing the same. To witness your community forgetting to celebrate, fumbling with bragging, sitting with the tummy flips of owning their brags after a lifetime of hiding them. You're not alone and there's such freedom in that!

The joy still pours off the page, even with all of its imperfections.

Jealousy

Within the community, it's common to find people celebrating small victories and major accomplishments with one another. Raising a virtual glass. Dancing in kitchens across the globe to share in the celebration of others.

One more stellar benefit of committing to the #BragOutLoud movement is the shared joy of celebrating with the community. Nothing says you can't celebrate another person's brag. In fact, I insist that you do. Respond to a member's brag with your own quick celebrations: "Dancing with you!" "Sipping my coffee in celebration for you." "Over here, basking in your joy."

But what if—what if seeing someone else's joy causes jealousy? What if the #BragOutLoud makes you feel resentful of someone's good streak?

Great. That's part of the human experience. It's just a reflection of the culture at large influencing us before we even realize it. It happens.

Normalizing the #BragOutLoud movement is an act of subtly

shifting our own language to transform the wider world. We're addressing the very real and learned responses of jealousy, resentment, and disconnection, and with minor tweaks, we're refocusing on joy where we can find it.

So when the green-eyed monster of jealousy shows up, instead of hiding from it—create compassion. Compassion for yourself, for your long history of doing it this way. Give yourself a chance to be kind and forgiving to yourself.

You are this amazing human who has had years and years to develop habits and be influenced in ways you'd never expect. We are all there with you.

Seeing the #BragOutLoud about money, or a perfect date night, or the perfect parking spot may trigger something for you that's less than kind, and that's okay. You are just recognizing a subtle pattern, so you can change that. Start by being nice to yourself and acknowledging how you first felt, and then give yourself permission to change your mind. "Yeah, I'm jealous of her new car. I want that for myself *and* I can take two seconds to be happy for her."

Those two seconds add up, until you can feel that twinge of jealousy and then switch into genuine joy and excitement for the other person. It just takes practice. Take a few days and brag only on what you're doing to enact self-compassion. Focus for 10 days on finding a tiny way to celebrate others in the group. It all counts. It adds up. This is how the movement changes the world—by changing you slowly and with love, ease, and joy.

You're just starting this journey, and no matter where you feel like you're stumbling, I am here to catch you. The online #BragOutLoud community is here to catch you, dust you off, and share—regardless of your brag or celebration's size, scope, or impact.

CHAPTER 14

THE FINISH LINE

We have covered so much. So much.

You are now armed with everything you need to spend as little as 90 seconds a day bragging, celebrating, and creating more joy in your life. You've got the easiest tool in the cosmos for battling your burnout and pulling more energy out of thin air. I promise you're ready.

My list of hopes for you is so long, it could fill another book. I hope that this process brings you more energy and a deeper capacity for simple pleasures. The ability to recognize all the things you do, every day, just to survive—let alone thrive. I hope you're developing endurance for longer-lasting joy. I want you to feel like you can be a little spontaneous. A little goofy.

I hope, from the depths of my big toes, you're able to feel safe. To feel like you now have a place to share. A community that encourages you to live and share your unedited life.

I am here for you. So is the larger #BragOutLoud community.

Knowing all you do now, about the process, it's time to try it yourself. Take 90 seconds and craft your first #BragOutLoud and celebration. Take the space provided to try.

My first #BragOutLoud is: _____

_____

and I'm celebrating by _____

_____ !!

Now, head to the #BragOutLoud community and post a picture of this page (www.BragOutLoudBook.com/JoinTheCommunity).

If you're already onto your fourth or fifth brag, *great*! Now it's time to invite others.

Building a Movement

The shared accountability and growth found in reclaiming bragging and celebrating is worth its weight in gold. It can be interesting, as you start to embody the #BragOutLoud mindset (recognition of all your hard work and intentional pauses to refuel), how you're finding yourself less exhausted and more confident. Seeing how the world responds differently to you. Your friends may start to wonder why you seem more rested, less likely to be grumpy, or even more inspiring.

Inviting your favorite people into the #BragOutLoud movement is easy when you realize you don't have to convince them it works. All you have to do is share how you feel. If you feel more open, more satisfied, more energized—say so. Start to share what you've gained. Please, please don't tell them they need it. Instead, invite them to join a book club, or take a peek over your shoulder at the online community's look and feel. Speak from your heart.

Your language will have naturally evolved; you'll be speaking differently. Hopefully your inner dialogue has started to morph, seeking out the brags, the quick celebrations. Which means when you speak to others, the language you use will have changed too. Congrats!

The Language of Revolution with a Revolution in Language

See, I've always wanted to run the world, to start a revolution. At some point in my late 20s I realized that was a lot of work (and therefore less fun). So when #BragOutLoud came into existence, I realized: I could change the world, with a lot less effort and with way more success than I'd previously realized. All I needed was critical mass. A cultural revolution is surprisingly easy when it's rooted in joy and minor (but powerful) tweaks to language.

That's the thing about culture: It changes quickly when we share empowering language. Now you've changed your language, and you've morphed your own inner culture. Which means....

You are now a part of the growing number of people recognizing all the tiny things. You're now celebrating as a way to access more joy. You've made a subtle shift. You're changing the world with the rest of us and we're so glad to have you!

Set your reminders, start today, #BragOutLoud as often as you can—and don't skimp on the celebration. In the pages to follow, you'll find a quick list of the links listed throughout the book and more ways to stay in touch as you begin and continue through your own #BragOutLoud journey.

You are now a part of this cultural revolution. Welcome!

I've always had a hard time with goodbyes and endings, so I'll say this: It has truly been an honor. I'm so proud of you for sticking with it. You have a gift, a devotion to your joy that is stunning. Not to be too sappy, but I know for a fact you'll be successful. You'll run with this, set it aside as you need, and then come back to it.

You are amazing and I'm so glad we spent this time together.

Tons of love,

~Shannon

P.S.: You also made it to the very end. As a super-secret gift for reading the first publishing of this book, I'd love to send you a little something: a signed bookplate! All you have to do is register and I'll send one (for free) to you as soon as I can.

www.BragOutLoudBook.com/FirstPublicationBookPlate

ABOUT THE AUTHOR

#SHANNONTOWNSEND

In Shannon Townsend's debut book, *#BragOutLoud: The Simple Solution to Finding More Joy,* she tackles the social taboo of bragging. While working as a nationally certified sign language interpreter, she found herself sick and desperately needing a career change. When the same thing started to happen again in her next dream career as an executive coach, she realized the problem might have more to do with how she was dealing with the demands of a "busy"-obsessed culture and a distinct lack of time to acknowledge all the tiny things that make up the day. While living in Northern Colorado with her husband, Joe, and two cats, Darkrawr and Valeera, she began the arduous task of starting a not-so-secret cultural revolution. Armed with enough gumption to fail, she invited an ever-growing community to change the world with her, in as little as 90 seconds a day. Now she travels, speaking about the astounding power of #BragOutLoud, celebrating, and the radical shift that the world is craving. You can learn more about her work, the movement, and her next speaking engagement at www.BragOutLoudBook.com.

Further Reading

#BragOutLoud Headquarters
Command Central for the latest news, speaking engagements, and steps as the #BragOutLoud movement grows can be found here:

www.BragOutLoudBook.com

Inspiration
The place for updated lists of quick brags and free celebrations. You can also download gifs to take all the "find a perfect brag/celebration" guesswork out of your #BragOutLoud journey here:

www.BragOutLoudBook.com/Inspiration

The Community
Ready to join us?

www.BragOutLoudBook.com/JoinTheCommunity

Keep in Touch
I'd love to hear from you and, if joining the community is a bit too much, I implore you to reach out and share more with me personally. It might take a bit longer to hear back from me, but I promise I read every message as quickly as I can. All you have to do is send me a little message here:

www.BragOutLoudBook.com/PersonalMessage

Book Club
Don't forget, there are book study guides (and bulk book discounts!) found here:

www.BragOutLoudBook.com/FirstPublicationStudyGuides

Leave A Review

Loved this book?

You can help the first publication
by sharing your thoughts on Amazon.

ACKNOWLEDGMENTS

I'd like to acknowledge my parents, who instilled in me the gumption to trust myself; my brothers, who always know when to show up; and an extended family that is always cheering loudest in the room, regardless of the size.

Of course, my husband, whose faith and confidence in me never wobbled—I'm not sure how he managed it, but he did. I heart you.

To Jenni and Cherri, who looked at the first draft of this book and valiantly made sense of the rants, the many, many disjointed points, and all the grammatical errors. You rock. I couldn't have tried again without your stubbornness and belief that I was on to something.

To the team at Modern Wisdom Press, who jumped in to make me feel loved as I battled "being human and writing a book at the same time." You are truly gems, and we're going to change the world one word at a time.

And last, to the community of early adopters: I'd be lost without you. Your steadfast love of this tiny idea allowed me to become the woman I'd always been searching for. You all are a dream come true. I'll never be sure how I got so lucky, but I know from the depths of my pinky toes, I wouldn't be here without you. Thank you.

If I missed you, this one's for you: I flippin' love you and your love of me and this wild ride is felt every day. Every. Single. Day.

THANK YOU

As this is the first publication, I want to say—again—*thank you so stinkin' much!*

I'd also love to hear from you. Reach out—connect. I can't wait to hear how you're doing.

I'd also like to make two, okay three, requests. Care to help a gal out?

1. *If you loved the book, the coolest thing you can do is share with a friend.*

    You can send them your copy of *#BragOutLoud: The Simple Solution to Finding More Joy*, snag them their own copy as a birthday gift, or start a book club (there are guides and discounts available; look under Book Club in the Further Reading section). The key is to share.

2. *Leave the book a review on Amazon.*

    Leaving a review that states what you've gotten from this experience does more than just boost ratings. It could also spark a stranger to take a chance on the book. You never know, maybe you'll inspire someone on the other side of the world!

3. *Ask your local library to get a copy for their shelves.*

   If it weren't for my local library, I never would have had a chance to read some of my favorite titles or read books that have literally changed my life. Our goal is critical mass, and libraries promise to support that goal while supporting your local community.

Thank you again for taking a chance on this book, on the #BragOutLoud movement, and on yourself.

Thank you.

www.ingramcontent.com/pod-product-compliance
Lightning Source LLC
Chambersburg PA
CBHW030120100526
44591CB00009B/468